Academia, Chernobyl, Expeditions and the Greeks

ACADEMIA, CHERNOBYL, EXPEDITIONS AND THE GREEKS

A Research Psychologist on the Move

Gloria Rakita Leon

FIRST HILL BOOKS
An imprint of Wimbledon Publishing Company Limited (WPC)

This edition first published in UK and USA 2022
by FIRST HILL BOOKS
75–76 Blackfriars Road, London SE1 8HA, UK
or PO Box 9779, London SW19 7ZG, UK
and
244 Madison Ave #116, New York, NY 10016, USA

Copyright © Gloria Rakita Leon 2022

The author asserts the moral right to be identified as the author of this work.

All rights reserved. Without limiting the rights under copyright reserved above,
no part of this publication may be reproduced, stored or introduced into
a retrieval system, or transmitted, in any form or by any means
(electronic, mechanical, photocopying, recording or otherwise),
without the prior written permission of both the copyright
owner and the above publisher of this book.

British Library Cataloguing-in-Publication Data
A catalogue record for this book is available from the British Library.

Library of Congress Control Number: 2021953398

ISBN-13: 978-1-83998-272-9 (Hbk)
ISBN-10: 1-83998-272-1 (Hbk)
ISBN-13: 978-1-83998-275-0 (Pbk)
ISBN-10: 1-83998-275-6 (Pbk)

Cover image: Cover photo courtesy of Gloria Leon.

This title is also available as an e-book.

Some of the names have been changed to protect confidentiality.

To those who paved the way

CONTENTS

List of Illustrations ix

Foreword xi
    Carol Amaratunga

Preface xv

Academia

1. University of Maryland Overseas Extension Division, Orléans, France   3
2. University of Maryland, College Park   7
3. Rutgers University, New Brunswick/Newark, New Jersey   11
4. University of Minnesota   21

The Russian Drama

5. The Beginning   37
6. Moscow Trip   39
7. Minnesota Bering Bridge Conference   45
8. Moscow, Archangelsk, Magadan Trip   49
9. Interlude   61
10. Moscow, Kiev, Chernobyl, St. Petersburg, Ryazan Trip   65
11. Interlude   83
12. Moscow and Minsk Trip   85
13. Epilogue   91

Expedition Adventures

14. Steger International Polar Expedition	99
15. Expedition Network	101
16. Soviet-American Bering Bridge Expedition	103
17. All-Women Expedition (Awe), South Pole	107
18. Sverdrup Centennial Expedition, Canada	109
19. Two-Woman Antarctic Traverse	119
20. Greenland Studies	123
21. Expedition Ice Maidens	157
22. Epilogue	165

Greece Connections

23. Athens, Peloponnese Peninsula	179
24. Athens, Delphi, Greek Islands	183
25. Athens, Corinth, Istanbul, Cappadocia	187
26. Interlude	191
27. Athens, Kephalonia	193
28. Athens, Temple of Poseidon, Marathon	197
29. Epilogue	199

Afterword	201
Selected References	205
Index	209

ILLUSTRATIONS

1. *New York Times* report of the settlement of my 1972 sex discrimination complaint against Rutgers University — 33
2. Presentation of the findings of my psychological research on the Bering Bridge expedition team members at Moscow Center in Fall 1989 — 93
3. Trip to the Institute of Ecological Problems of the North in Archangelsk in1990, hosted by Director Professor Anatoly Tkachev — 93
4. Standing with my driver and guide in front of Chernobyl Building No. 4, enclosed by a sarcophagus following the disaster — 94
5. Conducting an interview at a children's center in Ryazan, Russia, with a disabled participant in the 1992 15,000 km wheelchair expedition organized by eminent Russian expeditioner Dmitry Shparo — 95
6. Year 2000 Sverdrup Centennial Expedition group in front of their boat in Hourglass Bay, Ellesmere Island, Canada — 168
7. Lars and Guldborg inside the boat with a celebratory Norwegian *kransekake* Liv Dahl baked and brought with for our first evening together — 168
8. Liv and I departing the Sverdrup expedition Northanger boat site for Grise Fiord via snow machine and komatik (sled) — 169
9. My colleague and scribe Birgit Fink setting up for the interviews with the Sirius Patrol team members at the Danish military Daneborg Station in Greenland, 2012 — 170
10. Relaxing on the "retired" Brave Heart dogsled at Daneborg Station — 170
11. Birgit and pal in the dog yard at Daneborg Station — 171
12. Flare directed to Daneborg Station to signal a dogsled patrol team returning from the autumn journey — 171

13. Long-time colleague Anders Kjærgaard arriving at
    Qaanaaq/Thule, Greenland, at the end of an extended
    Sirius Patrol expedition, 2016 — 172
14. View of Danish military Station Nord, Greenland,
    outbuildings, site of second Greenland study — 172
15. Collaborator Jesper Corneliussen mentoring the Station Nord
    research participants as they practice a computerized cognitive
    assessment task during a 2014 organizing trip to the station — 173
16. Communications equipment at Station Nord left over from the
    Cold War era — 173
17. Traditional Saturday evening party at Station Nord with a mix
    of international station and summer workers — 174
18. Station Nord 2016 deployed work group at dinner — 175
19. The Ice Maidens, an all-military British women's Antarctic
    expedition team — 175
20. British military colleague Jodie Blackadder-Weinstein at
    Sandhurst in the main building where I conducted the
    interviews with the expedition team members — 176
21. Psychosocial disaster workshop sponsored by the Athens
    National School of Public Health with Greek and Egyptian
    public health and psychiatry participants, in Athens, Greece,
    2010 — 200
22. Psychosocial disaster workshop group gathered around
    Professor Jeffrey Levett (center), founder and first dean, Athens
    National School of Public Health, prior to departure for the
    official banquet — 200

FOREWORD

The life and times of Dr. Gloria R. Leon have been remarkable, if not extraordinary. As I reflect upon her scholarship, academic achievements and indefatigable optimism in this COVID-19 world of today, I am humbled to know Gloria as my friend and colleague.

Gloria's memoir is an eclectic collection of experience, reflection and wisdom, and is as enchanting as the woman herself. The four main sections of her book—Academia, The Russian Drama, Expedition Adventures and the Greece Disaster Connections—chart her life through her research and adventures, with meaningful lessons for young scholars and seasoned explorers. Her stories tell it like it happened, and they are also fun to read!

A clinical psychologist and researcher for more than 50 years, Gloria has accomplished so much for women in the academy, and she continues to make meaningful strides in the fields of gender and expeditionary psychology. I was just entering my first year of university in Canada when Gloria received her PhD in 1967 from the University of Maryland. A decade ahead of my generation, Gloria pioneered gender-based research in postsecondary and government institutions.

As in earlier times, women were not always welcome in academia, let alone in the esoteric field of expedition psychology that Gloria elected to research and study. Indeed, she had to overcome great hurdles, significant career setbacks and personal challenges. As she describes in her book, Gloria's sex discrimination case against Rutgers University in 1972 is a landmark example. As her career developed, she also had to understand and perform in the politically constructed, male-dominated realm of disaster management and space exploration. She never shied away from challenging tasks or difficult social histories.

Gloria has always had an intuitive, prescient understanding of things to come. Her pioneering work with Russian and Belarusian colleagues dates from before the fall of the Berlin Wall and the collapse of the USSR. Her research to investigate the psychosocial impacts of the Chernobyl disaster of 1986 on power plant workers and local populations was highly important. In her *mémoire*, Gloria reflects upon this time with grace and humor, recalling her newfound propensity for caviar.

In the years that follow, Gloria's positive psychology research would serve World War II concentration camp survivors and their families. As well, her psychosocial research with Vietnam nurses served to provide new insight and understanding into the impacts of post-traumatic stress disorder (PTSD). Indeed, she was among the first to focus on positive adaptive behaviors that can result from difficult and challenging histories. Her work in the field of positive psychology offers hope for the adage that *we are not of our parents, but through our parents*.

Gloria has always been generous with her time. Between 2003 and 2015, she dedicated time to work as a member of the board of directors and to chair/co-chair the Psychosocial Task Force of the World Association of Disaster and Emergency Medicine (WADEM). Her important contributions have enabled the delivery and adoption of lifesaving psychosocial supports and methodologies during and after many human-made and natural disasters.

Gloria's most recent research adventures, to name a few, have taken place with the NASA Human Research Program, including the SIRIUS-2020 Mars Mission, applications for the NASA 2024 Artemis Mission with research in Greenland to test a lunar habitat and a polar expedition study with the British military, also with implications for long-duration exploration missions. She continues to work closely with friend and colleague Dr. Jeffery Levett, National School of Public Health, Athens, to better understand populations affected by disasters, wildfires and earthquakes.

The "Noble Eightfold Path of Buddhism," as articulated by Sri Lankan monk and scholar Walpola Rahula Thero, provides a useful lens through which we can summarily view Dr. Leon's lifetime achievements. Her work has accomplished eight degrees of perfection in terms of (i) right understanding, (ii) right thought, (iii) right speech, (iv) right action, (v) right livelihood, (vi) right effort, (vii) right mindfulness and, last but not least, (viii) right concentration. In essence, her lifetime's work embraces the principles of high moral conduct and consciousness of the world around us—described by some as wisdom and mental discipline.

In word and deed, and at every juncture in her career, Gloria has made important contributions not only to her own field of expeditionary psychology but also to interdisciplinary fields such as biomedicine and environmental science. More profoundly, her life's work can be seen as an ardent commitment to address some of the world's most profound traumas: war, genocide and climate change. Simply put, Dr. Gloria Leon is a woman out of this world.

Carol Amaratunga, PhD
Dean of Applied Research (retired)
Justice Institute of British Columbia
New Westminster, British Columbia, Canada
June 2020

PREFACE

How did I end up in a professional career as an academic psychologist focused on research? The pendulum swings back and forth in terms of professional opinions about the relative importance of nature versus nurture on the pathway through which a person grows up and pursues a particular career. I know that throughout my life I have loved being physically active in sports and outdoor activities and always enjoyed adventure pursuits. One year when I was about 7 years old there was a tremendous snow storm where we lived, and the story of me jumping from the garage roof onto the snow drifts on the ground was a tale often told. Some of my expedition adventures, while not jumping into snow drifts, did indeed involve a bit of sensation-seeking in a challenging environment.

My interest in obesity and eating disorders: food was always very important in my immigrant family. By nature I was thin, and my mother and aunts always worried that I was "too skinny" and needed to put on weight. There were several times when a local doctor or a physician at the Mayo Clinic in Rochester, Minnesota, where I was taken for a physical exam prescribed a tonic (usually emerald green) to help me gain weight. However, I was healthy but just a finicky eater, and none of the tonics changed my eating patterns or my overall weight status. I grew up in Milwaukee, Wisconsin, at that time the center of beer manufacturing in the United States related to the large German immigrant population in the city. One of my aunts decided that beer was fattening, so when I was 8 years old I was encouraged to drink just a very small amount of beer. And I've been drinking beer ever since. Only in Milwaukee!

Thinking of my childhood and its influence on my professional interests in stress and coping in disasters and other extreme environments, my extended family and all of their friends emigrated from the former Soviet Union in the period after Word War I. My parents sometimes recounted the very traumatic experiences they or our relatives endured at the hands of the Cossacks or others in their village. Their immigrant status certainly had an impact on me in terms of personally experiencing the pressures of being a member of an often-discriminated-against outgroup. The usual immigrant tale of the importance my parents and others conveyed of doing well in school and the pride that came from academic achievements were always there.

Also, I remember World War II very well. I was 6 years old when Pearl Harbor happened, and I still can visualize my extended family tearfully together at my grandparents' house listing all of the sons and nephews who would enlist or be called up to fight. On the other hand, seeing these older male cousins in their impressive uniforms was very exciting. Over time and with some of their help, I acquired a collection of uniform patches from every one of the US Army regiments. When my cousins returned after the war, I was quite interested in listening to their comments about their extremely difficult experiences, including one cousin who had been a prisoner of war in Germany.

The situation in our family at the end of the war also remains as a vivid memory. I remember my father sitting on the floor in mourning and crying when he received word that most of his immediate family in what is now Ukraine were killed by Ukrainians and German soldiers during the war. The only two brothers and a sister who had served in the Soviet army survived. He spent a great deal of effort trying to locate any extended relatives and routinely sent packages of food and clothing to all those who still lived there. He was the first person in Milwaukee who was able to figure out the system to obtain visas for relatives to visit and later emigrate when it was possible for people to leave Russia. My overall interest in international activities stemmed in part from ongoing discussions about the status of the population in Europe and other countries, and my parents' involvement in different immigrant political and social organizations.

My specific focus on a psychology career began when I took a speech class in high school and decided to do the required paper and presentation on schizophrenia. I found the topic of mental illness to be fascinating and decided very quickly to pursue a university degree in psychology. My strong interest in psychology and specifically clinical psychology never changed, and I knew soon after I entered the university that I wanted to continue past my undergraduate work and obtain an advanced degree. As an undergraduate, I greatly admired the graduate teaching assistants and yearned for the time when I as well could teach others about psychology.

My interest in conducting research was fostered by my undergraduate advisers at the University of Wisconsin and the research requirements that were part of the undergraduate degree. The first project I assisted on took place at the local mental hospital and centered on assessing particular cognitive processes in schizophrenic patients. It was quite a stimulating and often horrifying experience to be in a mental hospital before the advent of tranquilizers, but I found the interactions with the patients I was testing to be quite fascinating. It also was very exciting to be involved in the process of conceiving a research project, carrying out the testing protocol, then doing the statistics and the writeup. I early on got "hooked" on doing my own clinical research as well as teaching.

My parents were tremendously proud of my academic accomplishments and, of course, that spurred me on to continue to achieve. I met my husband when I was a psychology graduate student and he was a medical student, and we both continued on trajectories formed by our professional interests. And as they say, "The rest is history!"

Gloria Rakita Leon

ACADEMIA

1
UNIVERSITY OF MARYLAND OVERSEAS EXTENSION DIVISION, ORLÉANS, FRANCE

1962

My academic career began in 1962 in Orléans, France, teaching a mental hygiene psychology course offered through the University of Maryland Overseas Extension Division. The university's regional division was located at Coligny Caserne, the US Army headquarters in the area. I taught a psychology course each semester for 2.5 years, holding class in the evenings, twice a week.

My sojourn in France happened because my husband was required to fulfill a commitment to serve on active duty with the US Army Medical Corps during the Cold War and was assigned to Orléans. What an amazing and wonderful assignment that was, considering all of the other possibilities. I applied for a teaching position as soon as I arrived in France. I really wanted to stay active in professional psychology activities, and I felt very fortunate that I was hired by the University of Maryland as a lecturer. This was a very tense period—the military draft, Berlin Wall construction and the war in Vietnam. However, being stationed in France was definitely not a hardship tour, and with a voluntary one-year extension, we lived in Orléans for three years.

The mode in that era was that you followed your husband wherever his career took you. By 1962, I had earned a master's degree in clinical psychology from the University of Wisconsin, completed a clinical internship at the Lafayette Clinic in Detroit and for two years worked part time as a clinical psychologist in Boston, first at the Massachusetts Mental Health Center and, after the birth of our daughter, at the Douglas A. Thom Clinic.

The students in the course I taught in Orléans were a mix of young men who had been drafted or enlisted in the army, career soldiers who were working on a college degree with thoughts of future job possibilities after retiring from the military and a few late teenaged children of military families. The students were very motivated to learn and do well, and teaching this diverse group of students was very enjoyable. However, after a period of time during the winter, I usually returned home after class with an absolutely splitting headache and feeling rather ill.

As a psychologist, I thought my symptoms were a stress reaction caused by lecturing and taking questions over a two-plus-hour period. Eventually, I was able to figure out what the problem was—carbon monoxide! My class was held in one of the quonset huts on the Caserne complex, and the heating was provided by a kerosene space heater. The lectern I used was situated right next to the heater in a poorly ventilated room. When I moved the heater to another place in the room and of course away from the students, voila!, my headaches and malaise disappeared. This was probably one of the quickest psychological therapy interventions ever accomplished.

However, dealing with the students' psychological needs was another story, especially in a course titled Mental Hygiene. Over time, a number of students approached me after class to talk, hesitantly at first, about some of their own psychological problems. So many who talked to me about personal issues seemed to be lost souls—drafted into the military, far from home, extremely lonely and teased by their barrack mates for being "bookies," that is, reading books and interested in intellectual pursuits. An army psychiatrist at the hospital was the only psychological counseling help on base, but his focus was on severe psychopathology. For the most part, these guys simply were dealing with adjustment problems in an environment they had been thrown into.

There was one young man I was quite concerned about who talked with me a number of times; he obviously was very distressed. He appeared to be in a panic situation because he was constantly surrounded by so many men. I suggested that he consult with the psychiatrist and then let me know how he was doing. But to my shock and dismay, instead of providing some counseling, the psychiatrist immediately transferred him out of the unit, and he was shipped back to the United States the very next day. He was even more distressed by this seemingly punitive outcome, as was I.

The assassination of President Kennedy occurred while we were living in Orléans. With the time difference, it was evening in France; we were dining with friends at a restaurant when suddenly word started circulating from table to table about a shooting. The exact details were not entirely clear at first. The French had such a strong fondness for the Kennedy family, and there was so much disbelief and distress communicated throughout the room.

Two days later, when I was walking to the Army Caserne, there were small American flags everywhere, hanging from the windows of the city apartment buildings. Across the street from the Casern, someone had placed a loudspeaker at their window and "The Star-Spangled Banner" was being played over and over again. Local people stopped Americans on the street to say how sad they felt. There was a real feeling of anguish on the streets, as people tried to process this terrible event.

Overall, the period of time we spent in Orléans was a wonderful experience, and for so many reasons. I just loved living in France. We had rented the upstairs apartment of a two-story house in an ordinary French neighborhood, and I did my daily grocery shopping the same as everyone else in the neighborhood, carrying my wicker shopping basket and wearing my sturdy French walking shoes. I took French classes offered at the army base, and I was diligent in studying every day until I had some fluency in conversational French. When one needs to speak to someone at a local store, learning French has a purpose, and it made it easier to remember words that you knew you actually would need to use. And, of course, there was the incredibly delicious food and the opportunity to travel to other countries in Europe. These were all memorable experiences. But after three years, it was time to go home.

2
UNIVERSITY OF MARYLAND, COLLEGE PARK

1964

We moved to the Washington, DC, area in October 1964 with a second child, a son born the previous year. My husband was assigned to the Walter Reed Army Institute of Research. This assignment worked out extremely well in terms of my career. Before we departed from France, I had been accepted into the PhD program in mental health psychology at the University of Maryland, and I resumed my formal academic training the spring semester of 1965. I was so happy to be a student again in a graduate program. It eased a long-standing underlying current of dissatisfaction that I had not completed a doctoral degree. I had a full schedule of courses, and I immediately began to consider a topic for my PhD dissertation research. Because of my prior clinical experience, I was awarded a graduate assistantship to supervise students in the program on psychological test interpretation.

I was very fortunate to have an excellent advisor, Professor Leo Walder, who was totally understanding of the demands of juggling family and academic responsibilities. He really facilitated the different academic "hoops" I needed to pass through to have my dissertation idea accepted by the departmental graduate committee and to receive waivers on several required courses that covered material and experiences I already had. Leo also made sure I had shared office space in an adjoining building where I could work undisturbed. Having a mentor like Leo certainly made a major difference in my progress through the doctoral program.

During my second year in the program, I was asked by some of the graduate students in the department to head a graduate student committee to meet with the faculty; there were a number of grievances regarding course requirements and the crucial seven preliminary examinations that had to be passed for the doctoral degree. (I was a few years older than the average student, so I guess that is what gave me the authority.)

Because there was so much riding on passing these particular examinations, the "prelims" were a major source of stress for all graduate students, and a frequent topic of conversation. In order to be accepted as a doctoral candidate, all seven exams, each covering a different domain of psychology, had to be passed with only one failure allowed per exam. Students were required to take all seven exams in the same week, so the pressures were enormous. We had a number of meetings with the faculty, and there were some compromises made in terms of course requirements but not on the prelims.

Despite the "grind" of graduate training or maybe because of it, there was real bonding among the graduate students. The recreation room in the house we were renting was large enough for holiday gatherings, and we had people over on special holidays. On the Fourth of July, several of my classmates gleefully set off fireworks in our backyard, much to everyone's excitement. Sandra Rosswork, a fellow graduate student, and I still stay in contact over this 54-year period. We have gone on adventure trips together and try to meet whenever I am in the Washington area.

The coursework was interesting and also challenging. Statistics was my nemesis—it did not come easy to me. Also, I was taking statistics courses during the pre-computer days. We had to do all of the sometimes quite complicated statistical analyses using only a calculating machine with a hand crank. These analyses sometimes took hours to complete, and I am still awestruck about how relatively easy it is to use a software program that will quickly run the analysis and accurately spew out the information, assuming the correct data entry format is used.

Statistics was one of the required prelims. I did not pass this exam on the first try, and the pressure was enormous. If I did not pass on the second round the following semester, I would be dropped from the doctoral program. So good memory skills came into play. I literally spent months memorizing the material in my statistics notes and the course statistics books, and I passed the examination. What an incredible relief!! It had been a major effort of motivation and laser-focused concentration.

In addition to the prelims, the PhD requirement included passing two foreign languages. I chose French and German. I was fluent in French from living in the country for three years in a local neighborhood and taking classes at the army base. Also, I grew up in a home where my parents spoke Yiddish to each other, and I had a fairly good conversational facility of the language. Yiddish is essentially a less sophisticated form of German; with a fairly minimal amount of studying, I was able to pass that exam as well.

The philosophy of doctoral programs at that time was that the PhD was a scholarly degree; a person who earned the doctor of philosophy degree was an academician, that is, someone with broad knowledge encompassing many substantive areas. At that time and even many years later, people referred to universities as "The Academy." This orientation is very different from current approaches in the United States; the conception and associated requirements have narrowed considerably in terms of what a person with a PhD degree is expected to know and accomplish through their academic training.

Along with my academic activities, I had a family, and it was very important to try to have enough time to spend with them. Also, day care was a major challenge. Although perhaps sounding like this was the Middle Ages, there were no established day care facilities available, either privately or sponsored by the university. Through newspaper ads and references, I was able to hire a woman who came to the house several times a week while I was at the university. I also arranged for a woman in the neighborhood who did some childcare to take care of my son at her house one morning a week. (My daughter was in early elementary school at this time.)

My study schedule was totally rigid—child nap times and every evening after the kids went to bed were reserved for studying, weekends included. I had a coffee maker in the basement recreation room where I had my desk and materials, and coffee was a total lifesaver. But I remember several times during prelims and on other occasions when I simply was exhausted. I would take a nap stretched out on the living room couch while the kids were playing in the room; they were able to see me and at least have my presence, even though I was asleep.

My husband was helpful with some of the chores, and occasionally my parents drove East from Milwaukee to visit us. We were very happy for their companionship and extra help, and the kids loved being pampered by their grandparents. On one of the visits, my father constructed the apparatus for the Bobo punching doll I used for my dissertation research; the topic was mother–child interactions with aggressive and nonaggressive children.

My academic curriculum included one seminar each semester, and I really enjoyed looking up the materials and doing the presentation; the back-and-forth discussion with class members was stimulating and fun. I also found it rewarding to write term papers on subjects that truly interested me and actually being able to look at the final written pages in front of me. Perhaps this was a good predictor of the scientific papers I would write later in my career. The positive feedback I received from my classmates and faculty on my seminar presentations solidified my goal to pursue an academic career when I completed my doctoral work.

In 1967, I successfully passed my final oral examinations, and my dissertation showing different patterns of attention to child aggressive behaviors by mothers of aggressive and nonaggressive children was accepted, 2.5 years after I entered the program. I called my parents as soon as I got home from the examination. Both were very proud and happy, and then my mother said, "Tell me again, exactly what kind of a doctor are you?" Medical doctors was the world she knew of. But everyone could relate to the fact that I had been given an award as Outstanding Female Graduate Student by the College Park branch of the American Association of University Women, thanks to the efforts of my mentor and friend, Leo Walder.

Leo and his wife Marcie threw a big party for me at their house after I passed my final requirements. The party was a wonderful finale after an arduous but very fulfilling pursuit, and I so appreciated their doing this for me. The fact that I had earned a doctoral degree also was celebrated in other ways by my extended family in Milwaukee. One of my cousins, who was a journalist, wrote an article about me that she titled "Doctor Mommie."

3

RUTGERS UNIVERSITY, NEW BRUNSWICK/NEWARK, NEW JERSEY

1967

Our next move was in 1967 to New Jersey, where my husband had accepted a research position with a large pharmaceutical company. I had begun making inquiries to universities and colleges in the greater New Jersey area for an academic position as soon as I knew where we would be moving to. I wanted to start off in a part-time capacity for a year or two, so I could spend more time with my family.

I was offered a part-time position as assistant professor in the psychology department at Rutgers University, Douglass College, in New Brunswick, and an additional appointment in the Rutgers Graduate School. Douglass College is the women's college of Rutgers University. The appointments began in January 1968. My primary responsibilities were teaching an abnormal psychology course and supervising graduate students on the psychological tests they administered to clients at the psychology clinic located within Douglass College. The agreement was that I would spend three days a week on campus. This started off as a very good arrangement; it gave me the flexibility to pursue other psychological interests on my own, working both on campus and at home.

In addition to mentoring students on their clinical cases, I began a research project on obesity, studying emotional arousal and self-control in relation to food consumption. I examined differences between the group that at a one-year follow-up regained the weight they had lost versus those who maintained their weight loss over that same period (Regainers versus Maintainers). I obtained the cooperation of Weight Watchers, headquartered in New Jersey, to recruit subjects for my research, and several graduate students at Rutgers assisted me on this project. I submitted a grant proposal to the United States Public Health Service for another obesity study following this same program of research; it was funded, and with this grant I was able to support a graduate research assistant, even though I was a part-time faculty member.

My graduate research assistant had an interesting background. She was a Berkeley product through and through. She grew up in the area and received her undergraduate degree at the University of California, Berkeley, where her father was a professor and the winner of a Nobel prize in physics. She told interesting stories of her father's dreamy nature, as he would suddenly be off in another world while at the dinner table, musing on whatever it is that physicists muse about. She was a bit of a lost soul in New Jersey after having lived in Berkeley all of her life; however, she was totally enjoyable to be with. In addition to mentoring her on academic issues, we developed a very friendly and fun relationship.

I wrote a daily questionnaire for these research projects that included a detailed analysis of eating patterns—items on food intake over the course of the day, emotions and daily events. Our findings showed that the Regainer group reported consuming food in a larger number of situations unrelated to feelings of hunger and a greater frequency of eating high-caloric snacks both in and outside of the home. Regainers also were more likely to report eating in response to a number of emotional states and feeling better after consuming food. Maintainers also reported feeling better after eating, but the emotional states that triggered eating were more specific to feelings of loneliness and boredom.

In contrast to the above results on the relationship between food consumption and specific emotions in obese subjects, a study I carried out several years later at the University of Minnesota with women who reported binge eating or were diagnosed with bulimia showed different findings in regard to the emotions experienced. Feelings of anxiety, depression, anger and disgust triggered the overconsumption of high-carbohydrate foods. During the binge episode, anxiety decreased but the other negative emotions stayed at the same level throughout this period; negative emotions and guilt followed the binge. Therefore, while the obese subjects in the first study tended to overeat and experienced pleasure in eating, subjects engaging in binge episodes reported primarily negative feelings both during and after the binge episode.

I took several months off for maternity leave after our third child was born in 1969. I then was able to hire consistent help, and I resumed my academic activities on the New Brunswick campus. After almost two years officially in a part-time status, I felt I was ready to move on to a full-time position. I actually had been working full time almost since the beginning of my time at Rutgers, although a significant portion of the work was from home and on my own time. My obesity research program was ongoing, I had successfully received federal funding for my research, and my teaching evaluations were very good.

A position opened up at Rutgers that I formally applied for, but another person was hired—a man straight out of graduate school with no teaching experience and no publications, major hiring criteria in research-oriented psychology departments such as Rutgers. I accepted the situation and remained in my part-time position; I simply continued with my own academic and research activities. But it was clear that my accomplishments were not valued.

The following year, the director of clinical training called for a long-range planning meeting and, in addition to faculty in the clinical program, invited Rutgers' psychology faculty from other psychology areas to attend. At one point, he mentioned a sum of money that was to go toward my salary. Most people including myself were quite taken aback when the newly hired clinical faculty person shouted out, "That money was promised to me!" There was a hush in the group, and then the director said, "Oh yeah. OK," or something to that effect. This meant that either I would have to take a still lower salary or perhaps there would not be enough funds left in the budget to keep me on.

I sat through the rest of the meeting in a turmoil of emotions, totally humiliated, shocked and angry. Two of the faculty members from the social psychology department who were at the meeting got up and walked out when this happened. I drove home in a state of emotional chaos. When I got to my house, still in formal dress, I walked down the driveway to the street; I just ran as fast and hard as I could until I was totally out of breath, to dissipate the emotions I was feeling. It was all so unreasonable and devastating to be treated that way, and especially in a public forum. Also, this new person was in the position that I had applied for.

After this incident in the spring of 1970, I was able to obtain a part-time assistant professor position in the psychology department on the Rutgers Newark campus, teaching an abnormal psychology course and advising undergraduate psychology students. There was an energy on the Newark campus located in the center of the city that was lacking on the grassy, small-city New Brunswick campus. The late 1960s–early 1970s was a very heady time; there were ongoing and increasingly intense protests against the Vietnam war and the beginnings of the feminist movement. Rutgers Newark was a very stimulating place to be.

The Rutgers law school building was directly across the street from Smith Hall, where the psychology department and my office were located. The law school faculty and students had a reputation for activism. One morning, walking to my office, I saw a white sheet hanging from the law school building with "On Strike" written in huge letters on it, protesting the war in Vietnam. (I recently realized that famed Supreme Court justice Ruth Bader Ginzburg was a faculty member of the Rutgers law school at that same time.)

On campus, there was a growing problem of bomb threats called in to Smith Hall. After a call, the entire building had to be evacuated, and, of course, classes were disrupted. There were no bombs found, and after a number of instances, a pattern was evident; the threats always were made for the same time of day, suggesting that it might be a particular class that was being targeted. The administration eventually made the recommendation that it was voluntary, but those who wanted to ignore the threat could stay in their offices or class. The rationale was that not responding with an evacuation would be the only way to stop the threats. I thought this was a good strategy, and I stayed in my office the next time a threat was called in. Others did as well, and eventually the bomb threats stopped.

During this same period, faculty were getting periodic messages to report any marijuana use in the building. While there often was an odor wafting through the halls near my office, I did not feel it was my responsibility to report anyone.

A university located in a large city presented some challenges. One day, a young man peered into my office, which was at the end of a fairly isolated hallway. I smiled and asked if I could help him with something, and he said he was looking for his brother. I told him that I had not seen anyone else around, but if I knew what his brother looked like and saw him, I would pass on the message. He gave me a few descriptive comments and left. About 30 minutes later, there was a loudspeaker announcement that there was a thief on campus with a history of violence who was robbing students. This was the exact description of the young man I had just spoken with!

On the Newark campus, along with my obesity research, I began an additional research project to assess personality stability and change following significant life events. I studied a group of disadvantaged college students who were in a special program at Rutgers Newark to improve their academic skills; I evaluated the group prior to their entrance in the program and again at the end of the academic year. I had a number of undergraduate psychology students working with me on both projects.

I also began to make initial plans for writing a case history book as a supplement to an abnormal psychology textbook. For instruction purposes, each chapter would be an example of a patient with a particular psychiatric diagnosis.

The idea of a case history textbook emerged while I attended the annual Eastern Psychological Association convention in Atlantic City in 1971. I was checking out each publisher's booth, hoping to find a case history book to assign for my abnormal psychology class. It was evident that no book like this existed, so I decided to write one. I was able to obtain case histories from several of the clinics and mental hospitals in the area, which I used for the different chapters. My approach was to include a section in each chapter describing the symptoms of the particular disorder, the treatment the patient received and research findings on current treatment effectiveness for that particular disorder.

It did not take very long before an academic publishing company was interested in the text. I signed a contract with Holbrook Press and worked on the book for well over a year. I wrote many of the chapters while sitting in the quiet of my local public library; my three days on campus usually were very busy with other matters. (Cut and paste had a real meaning pre-computer. I kept a scissors and Scotch tape in my briefcase to move written paragraphs around, as needed.) The book was published in 1974, and the first edition sold over thirty-five thousand copies. The book went through four editions; despite urging from the publisher, I was not interested in doing a fifth edition. It was getting tedious, and I wanted to spend more time on other projects.

I really enjoyed interacting with the Newark students, especially the several who assisted me on my research. It was very pleasant and interesting to have a small team of students that I regularly met with on research matters and also advised them on their future careers. The students involved in my projects had taken my abnormal psychology class and afterward asked if they could work with me. One of the students, Steve Kokourus, made coffee for me and the others every day I was on campus. It wasn't until the end of the semester that I found out that he never washed out the coffee cups!

I tried to be understanding when there was an issue that came up about a class assignment or grade, because most students were working often very tough jobs to earn money for college. Once, a student with a huge bandage over one eye came to my office to apologize for being late on an assignment. He said that he worked nights in a machine shop, and a piece of metal had flown into his eye, so it was hard for him to read. Another student told me that she had not done as well as she wanted to in her classes because she lived in a small apartment with her mother and numerous siblings, and it was difficult to find a quiet place to study. All I really could do was give them more time to complete their assignments. Course problems that came up with other students also were related to working hard with lots of difficulties to overcome.

I felt a huge responsibility to give my best at each lecture, because the students were so motivated and trying so hard to do well, often under extremely difficult circumstances. Also, I really looked forward to each lecture, to be able to communicate some new and interesting material. It was a good feeling when students approached me after the lecture with questions and comments.

In 1972, the Eastern Psychological Association convention was held in Boston, and I invited my cadre of four students to come to the meeting with me. I had submitted an abstract on my obesity research and it was accepted for presentation. I was driving a large station wagon at the time, and I was able to take the group with me. They made their own hotel arrangements, and as students often do, they all bunked together. My presentation went very well, and afterward, my students followed me everywhere I went, smiling and saying, "We're with Dr. Leon, and she got applause!" They were just so nice and fun to be with.

This was the early 1970s; the laws were extremely strict and the penalties were very severe for even minor marijuana possession. Rather to my dismay, I found out in Boston that my coffee-making student Steve had taped a stash inside his guitar to share with his fellow students. I only hoped they would use it up quickly to "destroy" the evidence! Steve was not exactly inconspicuous. He was tall and with Greek features and a beard that made him look like Jesus; he also wore a long blue confederate coat and high lace-up black boots.

Psychology conventions at this time were fairly free-flowing events; typically, people from different universities would host a university party in someone's room. Word would spread around with the name of the university and the room number of the party room. I don't remember which university party I attended, but I do remember sitting on the floor with the others in some room and flying high.

At the end of that academic year, my advisee Maria had a graduation party that my husband and I were invited to. There were many relatives and friends at the Italian feast set up in the family's yard—long tables and candles, light streamers and fantastic food. It was such a pleasure to see how proud everyone was of this young woman. Maria received a lot of kidding from her relatives, saying that she was now so smart and educated; clearly, all were brimming over with pride and happiness. Her immediate plans were to work for a year or so, save some money and then apply to a graduate program in psychology.

During this time at Rutgers Newark, I remained alert for any advertisement of a full-time faculty position on any of the Rutgers campuses. I focused on Rutgers because of my research interests. While I greatly enjoyed teaching, I also wanted to do research as an expected part of my job and not as a side pursuit, and I wanted to be involved again in graduate training. I felt I had more than enough proven credentials.

Over the next two years, I applied for two more positions that opened up at Rutgers campuses, the second position at Livingston College and the third at Douglass College. The same group of psychology faculty on the New Brunswick campus was making the hiring decisions for both of these colleges. For the Livingston hire, the demographics were the same—a white male who had just completed graduate school and had very sparse academic credentials, compared to my record. Douglass College, after turning me down for the position, later hired two women in temporary positions after I filed my complaint.

Following this third time when I was not hired, I truly felt that I simply could not accept this situation anymore without fighting back. I had worked too hard, sacrificed so much in graduate school and beyond to balance family and academic pursuits, and I had accomplished a great deal. I had to do something about this and fight back! I knew this was the only way I could live with myself. And at that specific time, in 1972, there now was a way to fight back. I knew that it would not be pleasant and the outcome was not clear, but I had to try.

The leverage that I now had was the fact that in June 1972, Title IX, the federal civil rights law, technically Title IX of the Education Amendments of 1972, was passed. This law states in part that there should be no exclusion based on sex under any educational program receiving federal financial assistance. Passage of Title IX resulted in major civil rights advances: women's sports at universities were officially recognized and funded, and discrimination in the hiring of faculty, staff and other positions was prohibited by law, with a penalty of losing federal funding. The timing of the third denial of a full-time faculty position at Rutgers coincided with the passage of Title IX; this gave me the mechanism and the power to fight back at what I considered to be blatant sex discrimination.

I contacted the Newark branch of the US Equal Employment Opportunity Commission (EEOC) to discuss my situation. Paula Roberts, one of the attorneys at EEOC, said she would take on my case, and we worked together to document as many details as possible to file a complaint under Title IX. For me, this was both an energizing and a humiliating experience—dealing with the publicity and my pictures in the local papers, people avoiding me at the Eastern Psychological Association conference held during this time, sympathetic looks by relatives and neighbors, and just the frustration of working so hard and yet being in this situation. The woman dean of Douglass College (the Rutgers women's college) was quoted in the local paper stating that my suit was "clearly ridiculous" and that I was "clearly outdone in qualification competition."

Colleagues whom I thought were friends stood by Douglass College's decision not to offer me the position. The director of clinical psychology at Rutgers, when confronted with letters of recommendation he had written on my behalf for other purposes, told my lawyer Paula that he was just being "a nice guy" and didn't really mean what he had written. However, my complaint was backed by the local National Organization for Women (NOW) and the faculty subcommittee of the Rutgers Newark Women's Caucus.

The EEOC filed a complaint against Rutgers University with the State Division of Civil Rights, at their Newark Headquarters. The Division reviewed my complaint and ruled that there was "probable cause" that I was discriminated against on the basis of my sex. Following this ruling, a hearing was held at the State Division of Civil Rights offices. I testified for over three hours at the hearing, going over the history of the job denials. A private lawyer who simply listened to the hearing was the only representation from Rutgers. After the first day of the hearing, Sylvia Pressler, the hearing officer, broadened the complaint against Rutgers University to include a second "probable cause," that I was discriminated against because I was a married woman with children. I had not expected this addition to the case, and I was very pleased that the hearing officer took this step on her own.

Given these two probable cause rulings, I was very hopeful that Rutgers would agree to hire me in a full-time faculty position, and I was willing to take a position at any of the Rutgers campuses. My lawyer tried to work this out before the next scheduled hearing, but from the university president on down, they dug in their heels. Their argument was that giving in to the discrimination suit would infringe on their academic freedom. Their lawyer made it very clear that they were willing to fight the case all the way up to the US Supreme Court. Therefore, by filing the complaint,

I effectively ended any possibility of a faculty position anywhere else in New Jersey. I was the troublemaker.

While the suit was being processed, my husband was offered a faculty position at the University of Minnesota. It was an excruciating decision, whether to move from a place where otherwise we were very happy, or stay, knowing that my academic career in the area was finished. Eventually, we decided to move to Minnesota, but the case against Rutgers still needed to be settled.

My lawyer Paula Roberts and staff at the Division of Civil Rights negotiated with lawyers representing Rutgers for a compromise settlement. I told my "team" that I would only agree to a settlement that would further the cause for all women in academia. After much back and forth, while the university denied bias, a consent settlement was reached. The agreement was negotiated by Raymond Nobles, the deputy attorney general for the State of New Jersey, representing both the State and me. Although the entire complaint process was very difficult, I was satisfied that the settlement that was reached would be of help to other faculty women.

Rutgers agreed that twice a year for the next five years, they would submit to the Division of Civil Rights the employment records of all faculty applicants. Also, each academic department on all campuses was required to maintain "affirmative action program" files on each person hired for two years after each position was filled. The affirmative action program was defined as the university's plan for maintaining equal opportunities for faculty and staff, regardless of race, sex or age; the plan would be monitored by the university's affirmative action officer. In practice, "equal opportunities" required that a certain number of positions had to be filled by equal-opportunity candidates in every department and on all of Rutgers campuses.

As part of the settlement, I wanted to be awarded a symbolic financial amount. While I had asked for a full year's salary, I agreed to the sum of $6,400, which was a little over half of what I would have been paid as a full-time assistant professor. (After all, I wasn't doing this for the money, and I donated $2,000 from this sum to the NOW. The settlement included a non-retaliation clause mandating that the suit be expunged from my employment records.)

My comment to the media after the settlement was announced was that for the first time, Rutgers, the State University of New Jersey, has agreed to be accountable to the State for its hiring practices. The settlement was publicized in the *New York Times* and local papers. The headline in the

New York Times was "Rutgers Gives Rights Unit Power to Oversee Hiring" (August 10, 1973).

This indeed was a very bittersweet "victory." I won the battle but lost the war because we would not have moved if I had secured a faculty position. And I was out of a job. We had family and friends in the New Jersey area, and we loved the first house we ever owned. On the other hand, we were pleased to be relocating to the Midwest, close to my family in Milwaukee, and the University of Minnesota is a prestigious university. But the move turned out to be particularly hard on our eldest daughter, who was 14 years old at the time and had a circle of good friends. We learned how difficult it was for a young teenager to come into a new school, not knowing anyone, and then trying to establish new friendships.

Today, so many years later, when I tell some of my students what the situation was like at that time, they are incredulous. The Rutgers graduate psychology program did not admit married women students; the underlying reason was that they might become pregnant and drop out of the program. If there was an incident of or continuing sexual harassment, there was no formal office within the university to deal with this situation. In terms of my own status, I was viewed as the dilettante housewife who was not serious about an academic career and, therefore, a part-time position without any job security was just right. Even some of the women faculty at Douglass College felt that it was appropriate for me to choose between being single with a career or being married and part-time. That you could not have it all.

Another sexist issue women had to deal with at the time, and in my experience for years thereafter, related to staying at a hotel. Simply checking in or walking around a hotel lobby while at a conference often elicited strange looks from the staff; it seemed they were thinking about prostitution. After experiencing a number of incidents when I was viewed with suspicion, I always made sure to pick up my conference identification badge as soon as possible, and I wore the badge at all times.

Several years later when I was on the faculty at the University of Minnesota, one of my women students and I were at the Midwest Psychological Association convention in Chicago. We went over to the hotel across the street from where we were staying to look for some of the other Minnesota students who were at the conference. We were stopped as soon as we walked through the door; the hotel manager asked us for the reason we were entering the hotel. Only after I said we were there for a conference did he move away and allow us to enter.

4
UNIVERSITY OF MINNESOTA

1974

When we first arrived in Minnesota, I was able to find a part-time clinical psychologist position at a behavior modification clinic, but I really wanted to get back to doing research. After six months of clinical work, there was an opening for a behavioral psychologist on a cardiovascular disease project at the University of Minnesota in the department where my husband had his appointment. I was hired for this "soft money" research associate position, but my heart was still set on a formal academic career. Also, the irony of the situation was that after all of my trials and travails at Rutgers, the head of the department made it very clear that he would not support having a married couple in his department in permanent positions, even though my husband worked on other projects and did not have any supervisory authority over me.

The first opportunity for a potentially stable position at the "U" arose in 1974 when I applied for and was hired as an assistant professor in the medical school in the Department of Psychiatry, Division of Health Care Psychology. This was primarily a clinical appointment in the Children's Unit. My major responsibility was to do psychological test assessments; however, I contributed to other professional activities in the department and continued with my obesity research. Now I was in a full-time faculty position, and it was such a contrast in comparison to Rutgers to work with faculty and staff who were very welcoming of my presence and respectful of my knowledge.

There was a great deal of communication between the health care psychology faculty in the medical school and the faculty across campus in the psychology department in the College of Liberal Arts (CLA). I got to know the CLA psychology faculty quite well. However, I still longed for a position where I could do teaching and research, and I was uncomfortable with the friction between psychiatry and health care psychology in the medical school.

Fortunately, during that first year in the Department of Psychiatry, the CLA psychology department had a position opening; they were recruiting for an assistant professor with a specialization in child psychology. Jim Butcher, Director of Clinical Psychology and Minnesota Multiphasic Personality Inventory (MMPI) expert, knew of my academic interests and strongly encouraged me to apply for the position. Several other faculty members in the department were very supportive as well.

I could not believe that it might be possible to finally realize my dream of an academic career; also, I felt this would be my very last opportunity to secure an academic position. I was terrified that irrespective of the non-retaliation clause someone would find out about my suit at Rutgers. Then, of course, no one would want to hire a "troublemaker."

I applied for the position and was invited for formal interviews and to give the usual "job talk." I focused my presentation on my mother–child dissertation research and the behavioral coding system I developed to document interactions between the mother and her child. The talk went very well and I was offered an assistant professor tenure track position. To my surprise and delight, I was also appointed assistant director of clinical psychology, to work with Jim Butcher on the graduate clinical program. There was only one woman on the faculty in the department at the time I was hired. I truly could not believe my good fortune.

However, my being hired was not without some controversy. One of the assistant professors in the department in the industrial/organizational area found out that my salary offer was $3,000 above his current salary, even though he had been on the faculty for three years at that point. He was very angry about this disparity. Other faculty also became upset about this salary issue and confronted the department chairman who had made the salary offer to me. They were not angry that I was hired; their issue was only about the salary. The resolution was that every faculty member in the department received a $3,000 raise! It definitely was a good, but rather uncomfortable, way for me to solve the problem.

My new position in the CLA psychology department included teaching an advanced abnormal psychology course open to undergraduate and graduate students, although my primary activities were with the clinical graduate program. I had my first experience doing administrative work, and I just loved everything I was doing. The psychology department was relatively small at that time, and there was a very nice collegial atmosphere that included monthly faculty lunches, gatherings at people's houses and summer canoe trips and picnics with the graduate students.

The clinical program had a large number of students enrolled at that time, and there was a great deal of external financial support from a National Institute of Mental Health (NIMH) training grant—18 stipends per year and some administrative costs. We admitted 12 students a year and supported them through the training grant; we allocated the rest of the stipends and some graduate assistantships to advanced students.

I interacted with the clinical graduate students in a number of ways, teaching therapy-oriented courses, advising them on their course work and monitoring their progress related to their clinical training. I was in charge of the clinical practicum, and each year I collaborated with the psychology staff of clinics in the area to place students in facilities where they would receive good clinical supervision.

My recurring meetings with psychologists in the community opened up an entirely new network of professional relationships. Jim Butcher and I went to the Minneapolis Veteran Administration (VA) Hospital once or twice a year to hear evaluations of the progress of our students on their practicum assignments. In winter, I loaded my skis and a change of clothes in my car, and after the meeting, I treated myself to a few hours of downhill skiing at a nearby ski area. The Minnesota slogan, "Embrace the Winter," is really true.

After two years on the psychology faculty, I was promoted to associate professor with tenure and also associate director of the clinical psychology program. This was an absolutely amazing passage for me, and it so confirmed my own beliefs in my ability and that I had not wavered throughout all of the difficulties at Rutgers. My research activities during this period advanced on two separate tracks: the first, studies of eating disorders, now including research on anorexia nervosa and bulimia; the second, studies of stress and coping in extreme situations—concentration camp survivors and their children and research on expedition teams. I also participated on a number of committees within the university and on NIMH committees.

In 1983, Jim stepped down as director of the clinical program, and for the next 10 years, I held that position. It was a great feeling each day to walk into my office complex and, in truth, feel the authority that I had and my satisfaction with the status of the program. We had strong clinical programs in both the adult and child/adolescent tracks and a great deal of professional recognition, reflected in part by national ratings of the quality of the program. I tried to keep all of the clinical faculty involved in program matters. I held monthly lunch meetings with the clinical faculty and annual long-range planning meetings prior to the start of the Fall quarter.

Of course, whenever a program decision is made, some will be in full support but others might disagree, sometimes strongly, faculty as well as students. I developed a rather thick skin to ride with the punches, keeping in mind my vision of the short- and long-term directions of the program. The clinical faculty included several international "stars" who sometimes acted like prima donnas, but that was just something I had to deal with. My contacts with the CLA and graduate school deans were always very cordial and supportive.

I must admit that the times when there was a significant disagreement with students on a program matter, the controversy was initiated by some of the women graduate students. For example, one episode involved continuous and increasingly angry pressure by a few students to make a very last-minute change on the preliminary examination date that other students were planning on. This was unfair to the other students, and I did not agree to change the scheduled date. These pressures did not happen regularly, but they did happen, and in many ways, they had the quality of a control issue with one's mother. I truly did not have these kinds of control problems with the men students.

Sometimes the research I was carrying out, particularly in the early period of my time at the "U," had a strong emotional impact on me. One of these projects was a community study of Holocaust survivors and their children. In the early 1970s, several studies and clinical reports were published indicating that not only were Holocaust survivors seriously disturbed, but because of their trauma, there was also a psychological transmission of disturbance to their children and even grandchildren. These conclusions were widely circulated in the media.

In reading this literature and noting where the study samples were drawn from, it seemed that there was a strong possibility of bias—individuals who were hospitalized with a psychiatric disorder or those seeking psychological help in outpatient settings obviously had significant psychological problems. But the question was whether this incidence of psychopathology would be evident in samples drawn from the community rather than from treatment facilities. It also was important to study both the parents and children from the same family, not just children of survivors who were seeking help for psychological difficulties.

I felt that not only had Holocaust survivors gone through horrendous experiences, but now they were being traumatized again, made to feel guilty that as a result of their experiences they had caused permanent psychological harm to their children and even grandchildren. Empirical research was what was needed. In 1979, I contacted Jewish agencies in three Midwestern cities. These agencies kept records of all of the World War II refugees and prewar immigrants they had helped settle in their city. I explained the rationale for my study and received excellent cooperation from all of the agencies.

The first step in initiating the project was to have the agency contact the people on their lists and ask them whether they were willing to have me or an assistant working with me contact them to describe the study. We followed up with a phone call to all who agreed to be contacted, and we explained that we were not going to ask them about their concentration camp or other wartime experiences; we were interested in their current functioning and that of their children. I chose a control group from the agency lists consisting of parents and their children of the same religion and European origin who had immigrated to these same cities a few years prior to the start of World War II. Using this comparison group, it was possible to control for cultural and religious influences in family interactions, eating patterns and social attitudes.

The majority of parents and their children whom I contacted agreed to participate in a home interview and complete several psychological measures. The research protocol I used consisted of several well-validated measures that assessed normal- and abnormal-range psychological functioning and current mental status. I also wrote Parent and Child versions of a Current Life Functioning form that included items about a number of family practices and societal attitudes. I did several of the home interviews; however, two graduate students in the clinical psychology program and a social worker in one of the other cities did the majority of the interviews. After each interview, we went over the instructions for completing the psychological inventories and arranged a time to pick up the completed forms.

One of the interviews I did with a woman survivor had a very strong impact on me. Her husband also was a concentration camp survivor whom she met in a displaced persons camp shortly after liberation; they married quite soon after they became acquainted. This was not atypical; survivors generally were attracted to others with similar experiences for social support and security, not romance. She said that now they lived a simple life; they were content with what they had economically and found pleasure in spending time with their children and grandchildren.

This woman had been incarcerated in a concentration camp for over five years. Although we told all participants that we would only focus on present circumstances, she began to describe how she had survived. She told me that her mother was imprisoned in the same barracks that she was in, and she knew that if she gave up, her mother would die as well. This was the motivation that kept her strong. She said that in the barracks she could see who would be likely to die in the next few days—it was someone who lost interest and became totally passive and withdrawn, and she did not want to let this happen to her. The coping and psychological resilience that she shared with me during the interview was just awesome. The combination of psychological determination elicited by the meaning she found in her existence, and the associated biological activation, seem to have kept her alive, and her mother as well.

Of course, survivors have documented that there were many situations that happened in the camps that a person did not have control over; for example, random shootings by the guards and typhus that raged through the camps, infecting people who were at the brink of physical exhaustion and starvation. However, finding a meaning in one's existence and following this meaning by one's behavior were experienced as significant factors in how people were able to stay alive. Personally, I simply could not fathom how a person could actually survive for over five years in these unspeakable conditions, but yet it happened. Of the group that I studied, over 33 percent of the women and 26 percent of the men had been imprisoned in a concentration camp for five or more years.

Our study results confirmed some of my hypotheses about the current psychological status of survivors and their children. We did not find the severe psychological disturbance noted in clinical samples studied by others. The mean scores of the survivor and comparison parents and children's groups were in the normal range on a measure of psychological functioning. However, the male survivor group reported a greater frequency of dizziness, fainting and restlessness, possibly due to severe head trauma suffered during incarceration. Many of the survivors continued to have intrusive memories about their war experiences—occasionally finding themselves thinking about the war, even when they did not want to. They felt they had survived the Holocaust because of luck, the help of God and others, and their own resources.

Because of the starvation experienced by the survivors, I was interested in looking at behaviors in relation to food. Our findings showed that some of the behaviors and attitudes that others attributed to the survivor experience were evident in both the survivor and comparison parents, and, therefore, not specifically related to prolonged starvation. Cultural factors were predominant—there were no differences between parent groups in eating patterns, food aversions and mealtime practices such as encouraging their children to eat all of the food on their plates. The women in both groups indicated that they cooked more food for each meal than the family could eat. In terms of attitudes toward their children, the majority of women in both groups and men survivors indicated that they worried a great deal about their children.

Similarly, we did not find differences in attitudes comparing the children groups. Both groups indicated that their parents had sacrificed a great deal so they could be successful. These findings again point to the influence of cultural factors rather than differences due to the survivor experiences of their parents. From a research methods perspective, the data demonstrated the importance of choosing relevant control groups.

I did a presentation on this study at a psychology conference in Israel. A number of professionals in the audience who were themselves survivors or children of survivors questioned my findings. Their comments indicated that they felt I was minimizing the experiences survivors had endured. I conveyed to them my own interpretation that irrespective of the horrendous experiences the survivors had gone through and the effects on their current existence, many had been able to cope with this trauma and lead productive lives. Moreover, there was no evidence in the study that their children were irreparably damaged psychologically because of their parents' experience.

I also stated that this was not to imply that no one suffered extreme and long-lasting psychopathology; however, it was important not to generalize from clinical groups to an entire population of survivors and their children. Also, it was important to highlight adaptive behaviors, as appropriate—processes of coping and resilience. I was relieved that the audience accepted my interpretation.

Peter Suedfeld, now a retired psychology professor and good friend, is a child Holocaust survivor. He is an excellent example of a person who was able to move beyond the trauma he endured and grow from these experiences, both personally and professionally. I never knew about his history until he asked whether I could suggest the names of professionals he could contact to write a chapter in a book he was editing, "Light from the Ashes." His plan was that each chapter would be written by a person who survived the Holocaust and later worked in a helping profession.

Peter told me that some of his experiences were similar to mine when presenting results from his studies of Holocaust survivors—others interpreting evidence of psychological stability or positive growth as a minimization of trauma. This can be very sensitive to deal with, particularly when facing a live audience, even one composed of psychology professionals.

Several years later, I conducted another study that had a deep emotional impact, research on Vietnam (VN) and Vietnam-era nurses (VN-E). The VN-E group served in the military during the war in countries other than Vietnam. At the time of my study, there was relatively little known about women who had served in the military during the Vietnam war; in fact, many were not even aware that women had been deployed to Vietnam. I was interested in studying coping patterns during and in the year after their military service, and also their current psychological status, 16 or more years following their return.

I heard about the Vietnam Women's Memorial Project through media publicity about their efforts to raise money for a commemorative sculpture in Washington, DC. The men who had served in Vietnam had belatedly received official recognition through the building of the Vietnam Wall, naming those who had died in combat. For the nurses, their sculpture would be their means of official recognition that they too had served, an affirmation of their contribution and a path to healing. (The group eventually was successful in their fundraising. A very moving sculpture of three nurses tending to a wounded soldier was designed and is located near the Vietnam Wall; the sculpture was dedicated in 1993.)

Many of the nurses active in the memorial project lived in the Twin Cities area. I contacted the local leader of the project, and she facilitated my contacts with other nurses to obtain their participation in a research project. As with so many of my projects, I found the personal interviews conducted after the formal questionnaire component of the protocol to be the most informative. In the case of the nurses, the psychological aftermath and coping methods they used often were in response to highly negative societal attitudes and behaviors about the war in Vietnam.

I did quite a few of the interviews myself. The women I met with were friendly and eager to cooperate. They shared many personal experiences in addition to the formal protocol, and later invited me to events in the area related to their fundraising efforts. Some of the experiences they shared were very sobering, and I appreciated their candor.

The majority of nurses in my study had their nursing school expenses paid for by grants from the military, with the commitment that they would serve in the Armed Forces for a designated period of time immediately after graduation. Therefore, many were straight out of college when they were sent to Vietnam. Along with their professional nursing efforts, they often served a role as big sisters to these young soldiers, indicating that it was very difficult to maintain some emotional distance from those who were gravely wounded or died on their watch.

Several of the nurses mentioned that the military stance was that they were medical personnel and professionals, and therefore they should be able to cope with whatever they were experiencing in their nursing duties. However, psychology tells us that it does not happen that way—depending on many factors, people find different ways of coping with stress; some methods are adaptive, others are not.

Because of the severe controversy about America's involvement in Vietnam and the growing protests demanding the withdrawal of our troops, the majority of nurses had extremely negative experiences when they returned home. One nurse told me she was spat upon at the airport when she landed in the United States. Others also told about the derision directed at them from people in the community. For many, these experiences led to severe discomfort in talking about their service; as a result, they were not able to process or overcome their feelings of helplessness and the trauma of treating severely wounded and dying young soldiers.

Given the negative attitudes many encountered when they returned home, one way they dealt with the situation was simply not to talk about their experiences. "Stuff it." One nurse related that both she and her husband, who also was a Vietnam veteran, frequently had nightmares; one of them would wake up from a severe nightmare and just rigidly lie there. Neither spouse would acknowledge the nightmare or, at other times, share their difficult experiences with each other. Another told me that in later years, even when she was in therapy for depression, she never told her therapist that she had served in Vietnam. Clearly, a person is not able to deal with and overcome trauma if, for whatever reason, they are holding in and cannot talk about these experiences.

The formal results of the study showed that there was a relationship between the emotional reactions and coping methods the nurses used while in Vietnam and their current psychological maladjustment. Reaction patterns in Vietnam such as anxious thoughts, self-blame, withdrawal from others and not expressing their feelings were associated with poor psychological functioning at the current time. Coping methods such as humor, helping others and including altruistic activities with the villagers were associated with positive current adjustment. Searching for the meaning of the events they experienced and other evaluation strategies also were related to current positive psychological functioning. Overall, seeking social support was a helpful coping method; however, many of the VN nurses avoided talking about their war experiences, thus preventing social support from happening.

My research findings across a number of studies of diverse groups have confirmed the findings showing that social support, humor at the time of stress to defuse the emotion of the situation and finding a positive meaning in the stressful situation one is confronted with are psychologically adaptive coping methods.

Over the next several years, I continued with projects focused on stress and coping in extreme situations, and identifying personality and behavioral predictors of the development of eating disorders. Securing funding to carry out research and supporting students to assist on a project is always a challenge, and this requires a great deal of time spent on writing grant proposals. It often takes several submissions and resubmissions, each time addressing the reviewers' concerns, before a proposal is accepted and funds are awarded, or sadly, the proposal is rejected. This process is a significant test of perseverance, tough skin and delay of gratification, hoping that in the end one will be successful.

I spent major time and effort submitting and resubmitting a proposal to the National Institute of Child Health and Human Development (NICHD) for a study of predictors of adolescent eating disorders, particularly anorexia nervosa and bulimia nervosa. Finally, I received a high score on the proposal, but there was one more hurdle—a site visit to my department by several members of the NICHD staff. Of course, I was delighted to get this far in the process, although it was really stressful to think of what was at stake—a final decision on funding following the site visit.

The NICHD team duly arrived and met with me and some of the graduate students working with me. They also talked with the department chairman and checked out our research facilities. Then I had to wait some more. Obviously, I was more than pleased when in 1990 I was awarded over a million dollars by the NICHD for a five-year longitudinal project on predictors of the development of eating disorders in an adolescent population of girls and boys.

I gathered a team of graduate and undergraduate psychology students to assist me on the project. Every fall over the course of the four years of data collection, we went to the junior and senior high schools participating in the study to administer the research questionnaires. Our team spirit and motivation as dedicated researchers were quite strong—it was still dark outside and quite cold when we arrived at the high schools in the early morning, wheeling dollies with a large number of boxes of questionnaires into the school buildings. We surveyed over nine hundred students in the first year of the project and followed them each year for four years, or until graduation. Four of the graduate students on the project based their doctoral dissertations on some of the data we collected over time.

Over the four-year testing period, the longitudinal results showed that girls had the highest proportion of disordered eating symptoms. For girls, a personality and behavioral characteristic of negative affect/attitudes was the strongest predictor of the later development of disordered eating. Because those in the high-risk group also reported other types of psychological problems, the negative affect/attitudes factor appeared to be a general vulnerability for any type of psychopathology as well as a specific factor increasing the risk for disordered eating. For boys, poor body image predicted disordered eating; however, boys' body dissatisfaction was associated with the desire for a more muscular body build rather than the thinness ideal indicated by the girls in the study.

Overall, my professional time was very busy and very rewarding. My eating disorders research expanded to the study of anorexia nervosa, and I carried out several research projects with colleagues at the Mayo Clinic focused on female adolescents hospitalized for the treatment of anorexia nervosa and a control group. Our findings showed that the anorexic group had an overall poor evaluation of themselves in their views about their body, personality and social skills. Negative attitudes and concerns about sexual issues were evident and may have been expressed as a fear of growing up or maturity. An extremely thin prepubertal body therefore avoided the pressures of dealing with sexual and other expectations related to chronological age. For some patients in a chaotic home situation, the control over the amount of food they put in their bodies was the only domain in which they had control over their lives. Fortunately, these attitudes and behaviors improved at the end of treatment.

In addition to the studies across the spectrum of eating disorders, I wrote a book on the treatment of bulimia nervosa that was published in 1983, and in 1989, the fourth edition of my case history book, now titled *Case Histories of Psychopathology*, was published. My moderate teaching load remained the same—an abnormal psychology course, a graduate course in theories of psychopathology and occasional seminars on other topics.

In 1987, I wrote a proposal for an NIMH research training grant for the clinical program; the research focus I designated was personality and interrelated factors in psychopathology. I was successful in obtaining an award for the four-year period from 1988 to 1992, with funds to support three students a year. I stayed on as clinical director until 1995; afterward, I spent more time on research and international activities, including expedition and disaster research. I collaborated for many years with scientists at institutes in Moscow and other locations in Russia, and colleagues in Greece and Denmark.

Dr. Al Holland, a psychologist at the NASA Johnson Space Center, became interested in my expedition research, seeing similarities to stress and coping on space missions. He invited me to be a member of a committee that would recommend psychological measures to evaluate astronauts and cosmonauts for the upcoming US-Soviet Shuttle/Mir missions. This first invitation initiated several decades of my participation on NASA and National Academy of Sciences advisory committees in the human performance area.

With the arrival of a Russian colleague to the University of Minnesota in 1992, I began collaborative research related to space suits—the development of a physiologically designed liquid-cooling warming garment, part of the space suit ensemble. Through these activities, I learned a new field, thermal physiology.

I spent the rest of my formal career at the University of Minnesota teaching and conducting research; while I officially retired in 2006, I continue to have an office in the psychology building and whatever staff support I need. Also, I am still working on expedition studies together with Danish colleagues, and currently I am collaborating with NASA colleagues on a NASA-Russian Roscosmos MARS simulation research project. I never tire of doing research.

On a personal level, my husband and I have maintained our independence in our professional pursuits, each of us acknowledging the demands and interests of the other. With incredibly important reliable household help, I was able to maintain travel schedules to conferences when our three children were growing up. The domestic and international travel for research purposes began after our children were on their own.

THE NEW YORK TIMES, FRIDAY, AUGUST 10, 1973

Rutgers Gives Rights Unit Power to Oversee Hiring

NEWARK, Aug. 9 (AP) — The New Jersey Civil Rights Division announced an agreement today giving it the power to oversee faculty hiring at Rutgers University to prevent discrimination against minority groups and women.

The pact, signed by the president of Rutgers, Edward J. Bloustein, and Civil Rights Director Gilbert Francis, requires the school to make detailed semi-annual reports of openings and applicants and submit background data on those hired or rejected.

"The agreement gives the division a broad review of personnel practices at the school," said Deputy Attorney General Raymond A. Noble, who helped devise the pact. The agreement was a by-product of the settlement of a complaint against the university by Dr. Gloria R. Leon of Scotch Plains, who charged she had been denied a position on the Douglass College Psychology Department faculty because she is a woman.

before and this agreement will probably help others who might have found themselves in the same position."

The consent agreement provides for the university to submit to the civil rights agency twice a year for the next five years the employment records of faculty applicants, and for each academic department to maintain "affirmative action program" files on each person hired, for two years after each position is filled. The affirmative action program is the university's plan for maintaining equal opportunities for faculty and staff, regardless of race, sex or age.

In a related announcement, the agency said it had reached an agreement with the Montclair school system, which had been accused by a local resident of discriminating against women in hiring and promotion. The charges were brought by Dr. Jane F. Robens, a Montclair resident who sought no job in the schools, but brought the

Figure 1. *New York Times* report of the settlement of my 1972 sex discrimination complaint against Rutgers University, giving the State of New Jersey the authority to monitor faculty hiring on all Rutgers campuses.

THE RUSSIAN DRAMA

5

THE BEGINNING

1989

It all started with a research project, a study of the 1989 Soviet-American Bering Bridge dogsled and cross-country ski expedition, an approximately 1280 km 61-day trek co-led by Russian Dmitry Shparo and fellow Minnesotan Paul Schurke. The Bering Strait is of strategic importance; the International Date Line, serving as the international boundary between the Soviet Union and the United States, is located in the middle of the Bering Strait. Because of the Cold War, the border had been closed for over forty years, separating indigenous families on each side of the border. The overall purpose of the expedition was to promote Soviet-American harmony by stopping in native villages along the way on both the Soviet and American sides of the Bering Sea. The guiding view was that the international focus on the plight of the people in the region potentially could open up the border area and enable residents in both countries to resume family ties and trade freely.

Co-leader Dmitry was a mathematician and a national hero. He was awarded the Order of Lenin, the highest civilian award in the former Soviet Union, in recognition of his numerous successful Arctic expeditions. He is an absolutely charismatic person and eloquent speaker. Through the force of his personality and commitment, and now with the help of his sons, he continues activities such as international youth summer camps in the Arctic to promote world peace. Co-leader Paul was a journalist at the time of the expedition; he previously had been the co-leader of the 1986 Steger International Polar Expedition, described in detail in the Expedition Adventures section. Paul continues his involvement in outdoor adventures, organizing dogsled and ski expeditions for able-bodied and disabled participants, many of which depart from Wintergreen Lodge in Northern Minnesota, owned by Paul and his wife Susan.

The Bering Bridge expedition was Paul's vision, which he pursued through contacts with numerous agencies. Dmitry later joined him on the project, and a Soviet-American team was formed. The efforts of both leaders to publicize the purpose of the expedition, and then as co-leaders to successfully carry it out, was a remarkable diplomatic feat. Official congratulatory statements were issued by Mikhail Gorbachev upon reaching the International Date Line and by George H. W. Bush toward the end of the expedition. Freedom of movement and trade agreements for the region swiftly followed.

The team consisted of 12 participants, six Soviets and six Americans. Each national group was of mixed gender, including both Caucasian and indigenous members. The expeditioners began their trek in the town of Anadyr in the remote Chukotka region of the Soviet Far East. They traversed the Bering Strait and then skied on to Nome, Alaska. The team flew from Nome to their planned finish in Kotzebue, unable to ski further than Nome because of deteriorating snow conditions.

Scientists from three Soviet and two American institutions conducted studies on the team, each with a different research focus. The Center for Disaster Medicine in Moscow studied a range of psychological factors; the Archangelsk Institute of Physiology, Ural Branch, metabolism and endocrine factors; the Magadan Institute of Biological Problems of the North, exercise physiology. The US Army Research Institute of Environmental Medicine (USARIEM) was interested in thermal physiology, cold adaptation and genetic factors, since each national team included both Caucasian and indigenous members. My University of Minnesota focus was on personality, coping and group processes. (Connections of one type or another sometimes can facilitate international research. I was able to obtain translations of the psychological measures I used on this project through the efforts of my Russian aunt who worked as a translator, other family members and friends, and Minnesota colleagues.)

Soviet and American research teams from all of the participating institutes met up with the group in Nome for the post-expedition studies and debriefings. I accompanied the group to Kotzebue and continued the debriefing interviews with team members at that time.

6

MOSCOW TRIP

Fall 1989

Professor Vadim Kostin, director of a disaster medicine center in Moscow, organized a *Beringov Most* (Bering Bridge) conference at his Center, held several months after the completion of the expedition. The plan was that each of the five groups that had studied the expeditioners would present their findings. Unfortunately, Dr. Mark Harmon, the USARIEM head scientist, was unable to attend. Traveling to Moscow at this still very tense time of the Cold War was an extremely exciting opportunity, and I was thrilled to have this chance. Dmitry was a key person in obtaining various official authorizations and working out some of the logistics of my travel to the Soviet Union.

The fun started when I got to JFK Airport to connect to my flight to Moscow. Through a communication glitch, I was under the assumption that Dmitry had arranged for my visa, but that was not the case and I was not allowed to board the plane. I quickly caught a shuttle flight to Washington, DC, and then spent two days languishing at the Soviet consulate there, hoping I still would be able to make it to Moscow in time for the conference. The visa came through literally at the last minute, enabling me to make a dash to the airport and fly to JFK. I arrived just in time to catch the night flight to Moscow.

It all happened so fast that I was not able to contact Moscow to notify them I was on my way, so I had no idea whether anyone knew that I was on this flight and whether there would be anyone at the airport to meet me. But as I stood in the passport control line at Sheremetyevo Airport, I spotted Dmitry's close colleague and fellow expeditioner Alexander "Sasha" Tenyakshev. Sasha literally jumped over the barrier between us, grabbed my briefcase, told the passport officer that I was a professor from the United States and it was okay, and rescued me from the line. All was well, and I caught up with Paul and the others at the hotel in Moscow, near the Moskva River.

According to Russian tradition, someone always carried my briefcase. After the first time or two when I said it was no problem for me to carry it, I accepted that this was a different culture, and, in particular, to have a man walk alongside a foreign woman without carrying her briefcase would have been considered the worst of impoliteness. So when in Rome, do as the Romans do.

Vadim, in addition to serving as director of the Center, was the head of the PhD granting Department of Disaster Medicine at the Institute of Biophysics and also active in the Soviet space program. His professional activities focused on physiological and hygienic factors to enhance worker protection, including research on the development of advanced space suits and other personal protective equipment. Vadim had an interesting background; he was born on a collective farm in Siberia, where his father was an agricultural worker and his mother supervised the dairy. He also had been a cosmonaut candidate and was one of the first chief medical officers on the scene in the immediate aftermath of the 1986 Chernobyl explosion.

The Center was built following the Chernobyl disaster. When I entered the building, the first thing I noticed was a marble bust of Lenin, about 1.25 m tall, placed in front of the opposite wall in the lobby. To get into the main part of the building, I had to show my passport to a security person, place my briefcase on the conveyer belt and walk through the security screening apparatus. Vadim's office was an extremely large room that included an oval table that could seat about fifteen or more people. (I noted the same setup in all of the other directors' offices I visited at other institutes—this was the main conference room.) Also, directors' offices still followed a practice from Czarist times—double doors for security. The reason? With two doors, those inside an office were alerted when the first door was opened, allowing some time to prepare or protect themselves before the second door was opened. Also, I realized that there was a listening device on the ceiling above Vadim's desk; whenever he needed something from the secretary, all he did was raise his head to the ceiling and yell "Svetlana!"

Based on my observations over several visits, I knew there was a KGB office located in the Center. This was a period of major societal control by the Communist Party. A Center staffer confided in me that every Friday afternoon he had the duty to give a talk on the advantages of Communism, which the entire Center staff was required to attend.

Vadim's office was the only director's office that I visited during the Soviet Union era that did not have an almost floor-to-ceiling portrait of

Lenin in the room. At a later visit, he told me that he had resigned from the Communist Party out of disgust with the politicization of the Chernobyl response, which was an extremely brave thing to do.

The *Beringov Most* conference was truly impressive, and there was a large turnout of professionals from Moscow and other cities. For our presentations, each of us used 35 mm slides and a long wooden pointer to focus the audience on particular items of interest on the screen. I had an excellent translator, and I easily got into the rhythm of saying a few sentences and then waiting for the translation before I continued talking. I fully enjoyed answering questions from the audience and tried to explain the rationale for some of the differences in approach between American and European research methods. For example, I presented means and standard deviations when I showed group data on the MMPI personality measure. The Russian presentations all showed individual data; they felt that averages/means were meaningless because there was no one person who had received those particular scores. There is indeed a difference in scientific method reflected here.

Overall, I had a true feeling of friendship and camaraderie with the people from this impressive Center and other institutes. The atmosphere was relaxed, and we did get numerous chances to present toasts to each other with the motif of *druzhba* (friendship) when we gathered informally. There were lots of laughs along with more serious topics. I spent quite a bit of time over the next few days following the conference talking with the other Soviet investigators, planning on how we could maintain research connections among our different institutions, all the time sitting around a large table drinking tea and sometimes a bit of cognac.

I was taken on a tour of the laboratories located on the lower level of the Center. There were approximately five environmental chambers, each replicating air pressure and thermal conditions of high altitude, deep sea or outer space, respectively. I saw a subject in one of the chambers, supine on a recumbent exercise bike; several technicians outside of the chamber were monitoring the procedure. However, while the Center was fairly new and "state of the art," I was surprised that some bathroom fixtures in the women's restroom were broken off.

The itinerary for this visit included some Moscow sightseeing, with five of us crushed into a very small Soviet Lada automobile. Since George Sweasy (a benefactor of the expedition, from the Red Wing Shoe Company in Minnesota) was the shortest man in the group, it was decided that I should sit on his lap because there was no other room in the vehicle. We both took this in a good-natured way. As we raced across Moscow from one place to the next, I had to duck my head in the car because of the low ceiling and the poor roads.

The Center also arranged for several of us to visit the psychology department at the prestigious Moscow State University. We were accompanied by Dr. Vasili Markov, a psychiatrist on the Center staff, and Kristina, my interpreter. A member of the psychology faculty proudly showed us a computerized version of the Lüscher Color Test. This measure is based on the theory that the colors an individual prefers is a reflection of their personality and/or psychopathology. One of the unique aspects that they were showing us was the ability to display this test via desktop computer, the creation of their IT staff. They were quite proud of this accomplishment, because this was an early 1990 era when computers were not widely available in certain settings.

The hotel we American visitors stayed at had its own personality (and challenges). My room was very comfortable, consisting of two narrow twin beds, a private bath and a nice view; however, the elevator was an interesting story. I discovered through trial and error that the ascending elevator only stopped on odd-numbered floors. Since my room was on an even-numbered floor, depending on my mood, I decided each time (rather than the elevator) whether I wanted to walk up one flight or down one flight, as pressing the number of my floor did not result in the elevator stopping there. On the other hand, the elevator did stop on every floor descending to the lobby. But then lo and behold, the last day when I used the elevator from the lobby, I had a new experience—I pressed the odd number above my floor, but the elevator actually stopped on my own even-numbered floor! A total mystery of Soviet hotel engineering.

The most interesting elevator event happened that evening when all of us were getting ready to go to expeditioner Dmitry and his wife Tatiana's apartment for dinner. Paul and I happened to get to the elevator door on our floor at the same time. He pressed the down button, we entered the elevator and saw a very serious-looking man already on the elevator. He was staring straight ahead and holding a huge silver platter with burlap thrown over a large oblong object with a tongue sticking out and part of an eye visible through the burlap. And then the elevator went up rather than down! I kept making sidelong glances at the platter, and when the man got off and Paul and I were truly on our way down to the lobby, with a tremor in my voice I asked, "Paul, was that a horse's head?" He said, "Yes," and explained that this was a great delicacy at Central Asian weddings, each slice washed down with vodka or some other alcoholic beverage. All I could say was "Eeeuw."

We all had a fantastic time at Dmitry and Tatiana's apartment, with delicious food and drinks that they could only purchase at special stores for the Soviet elite, particularly when hosting foreign visitors. There was music, laughter and lots and lots of heartfelt toasts. Close personal space is not a Soviet thing, likely due to many people living together in small apartments, so we all were in quite close proximity to one another. There was truly an emotional feeling of friendship and the strong wish to continue working together and seeing each other again. At this point, I already had made a commitment to organize a reciprocal conference on the Bering Bridge studies through the Department of Conferences at the University of Minnesota. So we did know that we would see each other again in the near future, and we all truly looked forward to that event.

7
MINNESOTA BERING BRIDGE CONFERENCE

May 1990

The Department of Conferences at my university took care of all of the arrangements, including visas, and I arranged for all visitors to stay in people's homes. Center director Vadim, Dmitry and Professor Anatoly Tkachev, chief of the Ecological Endocrinology Department, Institute of Physiology, Ural branch from Archangelsk stayed at my house. Several stayed at the home of University of Minnesota Russian Studies professor Adele Donchenko, whose office was in the same building as mine, and a few others were housed elsewhere. Adele knew our study very well because she had translated some of the questionnaire measures into Russian.

However, while I provided the conference staff with a list of participants and their home cities in order to obtain the US visas, the sparse emails back and forth suggested that it wasn't entirely clear exactly who was coming and when they would arrive via Aeroflot. As Adele commented from her own experience, "You never know until you see who walks off the plane."

I anxiously awaited a planned phone call from Dmitry when the group landed at JFK. Finally, he called. They were at the airport, but there was about an eight-hour delay before they could get a flight to Minneapolis. They were very tired, he said, but they would cope as there was no earlier flight I could get them on. Dmitry, as a true expedition leader, somehow led a mini-expedition into Manhattan until it was time to return to JFK for their flight to Minneapolis.

I waited at the airport with a psychology student who was helping me with the conference. I still was not sure exactly how many people were coming, and I had a rather overwhelming feeling when eight people got off the plane: Dmitry; Vadim; Anatoly from Archangelsk; Professor Asilbek Aidareleyev, Director, Institute of Biological Problems of the North in Magadan; Dr. Maxim Abramov from the same institute; two film producers; and the deputy mayor of Irkutsk Siberia, Anatoly Dormidontov.

Wow! Between two cars, we got everyone to the places they were staying at, and settled in.

The University of Minnesota conferences department did their usual highly professional arrangements. The one-day conference was held at the Coffman Student Union on campus and went off without a glitch. The conference also was reasonably well attended by university faculty and students. Dr. Mark Harmon from USARIEM attended and presented his thermal physiology and other findings; Russian-language students helped with the translations for our Soviet visitors. Vadim also gave a talk the following day in the psychology department on the Russian uses of a translated and modified MMPI, the well-known personality inventory developed through the Departments of Psychiatry and Psychology at the university, which, incidentally, the Soviets have used for screening cosmonaut candidates since the earliest days of their space program.

I had a big party at our house on the evening of the conference. My husband had been called up for active duty in the Army during the Kuwait Desert Storm, so I did all of the hosting. George Sweasy, part of our prior Moscow contingent, came up from Red Wing to attend the party. Dmitry was particularly intrigued with my daughter Michelle. He said that his son Nikita would be a perfect match for my daughter, and he wanted to make an immediate phone call to Moscow for the two of them to talk together. No time wasted! Michelle was not interested, and basically I think neither was Nikita, but for many years afterward, Dmitry and I had a running joke that we could be relatives some day. On the night of the party, George slept on the floor in my great room.

George had a private plane, and the next day he flew Vadim to Rochester, Minnesota, for an arranged meeting with the Mayo Clinic developers of a high-altitude pressure garment for jet pilots. The agenda was to have a conversation about each country's development of protective garments for aviation and space purposes. Also, the visit gave Vadim the opportunity to see the Mayo Clinic pressure garment.

Throughout this visit, our group had numerous discussions on how to maintain our research and personal connections, focused on applying American scientific methods to projects carried out in the Soviet Union. We also made initial plans to translate into Russian several psychological questionnaires that had been developed in my department. We talked about strategies for standardizing these Russian-translated measures by developing norms on a Russian population. This was a very interesting possibility that we pledged to pursue.

For the next few days, it was my responsibility to be the tour director, and with the help of others, we did some sightseeing in the Twin Cities area. However, the place that most impressed the Soviet group was the Old Country Buffet. They were amazed that it was possible to see such a variety of food and absolutely to take as many helpings as they wanted to. This was a time of considerable hardship in the Soviet Union, and the availability of this variety and amount of food was memorable for the visitors.

The last part of their visit was a trip to Ely, Minnesota, to the Schurke Wintergreen Lodge. I rented a large van from the university and we drove through some beautiful scenic areas on our way "Up North." Paul and his wife Susan were wonderful hosts for this overnight visit. Their rustic lodge overlooks a lake, and there is a large area for their many sled dogs. We followed our usual pattern of great food, lots of drinks and toasts, and general camaraderie. Most of the group were housed in adjoining cabins, but I ended up sleeping curled up on a very small love-seat-type bench in the lodge itself. No worries, we were all having a good time. And all these years later, I still keep the group photo in front of the lodge on a shelf in my study, right next to my computer.

On our return to the Twin Cities, we stopped at a McDonald's outside of Duluth. At first, I was asking each person what they wanted to eat, but then Maxim from Magadan said, "Gloria, no problem! Just order eight Big Macs, eight french fries, eight cokes and whatever you want for yourself." Great advice, and that's what I did. As we got closer to Minneapolis, someone in the group said, "Gloria, let's go to Goodwill." I don't know how they had heard about Goodwill, but they had, and they were thoroughly delighted with all of the bargains they found there. Next, we went back to my house, and somehow I got a roast in the oven; several helped out with the cooking, and we had a wonderful and warm final dinner together.

Dmitry stayed with another friend this last night, and others dispersed to where they were staying. We made final plans for gathering early the next morning to go to the airport as a group. As Vadim was just about to go through the Jetway, he whispered in my ear that he wanted to live in the United States. We had formed a bond that lasted until his death in November 2018.

8

MOSCOW, ARCHANGELSK, MAGADAN TRIP

June 1991

Vadim made all of the arrangements for my next trip to Russia. In addition to time in Moscow, I also visited the institutes in Archangelsk and Magadan whose investigators were part of the Bering Bridge study, making a global circle by flying back home from Magadan in the Soviet Far East to Anchorage, Alaska.

Upon arrival in Moscow, Vadim and his driver met me at the airport and drove me to my hotel. I was housed at a hotel that was just across a small park from the Center. I settled in and rested a bit, and then Vadim picked me up again a few hours later to go over to his house for dinner. I was quite tired after this long flight and not very hungry, but of course, I couldn't say no to the invitation.

Their apartment was on the upper floor of a typical large concrete Soviet-style building block. The main entrance was poorly lit and the elevator was quite dirty. (Apparently no one takes responsibility for the public areas; I found this same situation in other apartment buildings I visited over the course of my stays in Russia.) However, the Kostin apartment was very nice, including a large oriental rug hanging on a wall in the living room.

Vadim's wife Polina and their daughter Marya were both physicians and were very friendly and talkative. We had an excellent meal, and I answered the many questions they had about life in America. Polina proudly showed me English instruction books she was studying to improve her English skills and asked me whether she was correctly pronouncing the different words and sentences she said out loud.

My hotel room was a small suite with some basic cooking facilities. It was a hotel that I was told housed scientists working in secret areas! Outside of the hotel 24-7 was an obvious KGB car with two men inside; the passenger door was open and two red lights were blinking from the dashboard. Inside the hotel, a *militsiya* (policeman) stood duty in the lobby; however, all the people in the lobby including the *militsiya* stopped what they were doing and stared raptly at the television set when Cuban soap operas were broadcast around noon each day.

I brought some gifts for the people that I knew at the Center. This is always a challenge when traveling, choosing something interesting and useful, yet not too large, so all will fit in your suitcase. I bought small Panasonic hand calculators for everyone as a present from America. But Marc, one of the psychologists, said, "Gloria, you are bringing presents from America, but these are made in Japan." Sometimes you can't win!

My conversations with members of the Center proceeded quite easily. Most of the people I met with spoke English quite well, and Kristina, my fantastic interpreter, was always there to help out. (I now realize that I never knew her last name; usually the men were referred to by their family name and the women by their first name. Perhaps not that different from traditions in other countries.) Kristina was able to follow conversations by different people that might be going on almost simultaneously and clearly whisper the translation to me without interrupting the flow of the interaction. The Center discussions were focused on different research possibilities, with an agenda of ultimately submitting grant proposals to institutions in the United States that might be interested in funding international collaborative research.

In this time of economic difficulties in the Soviet Union, the various scientific institutes were eager for any type of international collaboration that, in the process, could bring in funds to support their institute activities. This topic was rather sensitive because of the Cold War; international distrust at high government levels was a significant reality. However, we clearly were not talking about the dissemination of any type of classified information.

One project that we worked out some details on was the Russian translation of the newly modified and standardized MMPI-2 personality inventory, recently published by the University of Minnesota Press. Prior to this visit, I had obtained a commitment from the University of Minnesota Press for some funds to award to the Center to carry out this project. The plan included both the translation and back translation for linguistic accuracy of the 567-item MMPI-2, and the collection of a stratified randomized sample of Russian groups to standardize the scale norms for a Russian population.

Vasili Markov, my escort on the previous visit to the Moscow State University, was placed in charge of the MMPI project, and Kristina headed the translation effort. Vasili was a psychiatrist and an officer in the

Soviet Air Force; his professional efforts included support of personnel in the Soviet space program and in other extreme environments. He spoke English fluently, and both Vasili and Kristina became my "team." We traveled together like The Three Musketeers both in Moscow and in other cities in the Soviet Union/Russia, accompanied by a driver and a local scientist if we were in another city. This was quite the royal treatment, and I really was not expecting this kind of attention.

Conversations with the Center group also evolved to the idea of writing a collaborative paper based on the Russian MMPI data that were routinely collected on the Chernobyl power plant workers, to be submitted to an English-language psychology journal. One of the points of interest someone in the group brought up was whether there was a change in the personality characteristics of the Chernobyl plant workers who volunteered/agreed to work at the plant before the explosion, compared to four groups who had worked at the plant at different time intervals following this incredible disaster.

I was given a file containing these MMPI data to take back with me to Minnesota to analyze and write up. Marc, a Center psychologist, was rather incensed that I had been given data that only the week before had been declassified from a secret category, but no one paid attention to his comments. The results of the analysis showed an increase in health concerns, depression and other indicators of stress over time, comparing the pre-disaster with the post-disaster power plant worker groups. There also was an increase in stress indicators over time across the four post-disaster groups, likely due to the continuing uncertainty of the safety of working at the facility.

On another day, Professor Olga Kosorenko, a chief psychologist in the Soviet space program, came to the Center to meet with me. Her activities included psychological support for cosmonauts in training and during space flights. Olga was interested in my activities with NASA and my other research projects; it was basically a friendly chat. At the time, I was a member of a committee chaired by Dr. Al Holland, a psychologist at the NASA Johnson Space Center, tasked to develop a joint psychological testing protocol for the Shuttle-Mir missions. Olga and I stayed in touch via email after this visit, and several times I sent small presents back to her when I met one of the Russian space researchers at a meeting in the United States.

The psychologists I met with in Russia had quite different academic backgrounds than mine: they all were medical school graduates. The Soviet medical school curriculum is highly specialized and students receive course work and clinical training in a very narrow track. Following in the tradition of the great Russian physiologist Ivan Pavlov, all of the psychologists at the Center were referred to as psychophysiologists.

This emphasis on psychophysiology was reflected in some of the Soviet approaches to cosmonaut selection, such as placing an applicant wired with numerous biosensors in a small chamber, simulating an emergency in the chamber and then monitoring both their physiological and the behavioral responses. During the Russian disarmament of nuclear missiles, psychophysiologists were also involved in monitoring the worker doing the dismantling, stopping the process if the worker's stress was at a level judged dangerous to continue.

The female staff at the Moscow Center were very busy, charged with clerical activities and serving tea. Irrespective of their position, the women served the tea! I noticed that the staff were using carbon paper to make multiple copies of whatever they were working on, as copying machines were scarce. There also were other scarcities and restrictions. Having a copying machine in one's home was not allowed, and there were no telephone books available during this period. One had to personally get the phone number from whomever one wanted to stay in touch with. Also, at that time there were only two phone lines into the entire city of Moscow from the United States. If I needed to make a call to the Center, I would do this in the middle of the night, continuously dialing the main number until I finally got through, shouting "*Eta Gloria, ez Minnesota. Vadim pozhalesta*" (This is Gloria from Minnesota. Vadim please).

During this trip, a driver from the Center took me along with Vasili and others to a large well-known Russian Orthodox monastery in the town of Zagorsk. The monastery was very beautiful and had numerous icons on the walls and lit candles on tables. Despite the Soviet Union still officially an atheist country, the service was well attended, although by older women and men. The priests were dressed in traditional black robes and high hats; all had heavy long beards. The attendees did the Orthodox sign of the cross and bowed repeatedly throughout the service.

Escorted by Vasili, I also visited the USSR Center for Preventive Medicine in Moscow to say hello to Dr. Nina Arkharova, who was a researcher within the Center's Laboratory for the Prevention of Coronary Heart Disease. Nina is the wife of Dr. Misha Arkharov, who at the time was on a fellowship in the Division of Epidemiology at the University of Minnesota. I also met with the head of the Center together with the head of the Group of Psychology; both described some of their ongoing research projects.

A side note: Misha had helped to translate some of the psychology questionnaires I used in my research, and he became a close family friend. Being quite large in stature, I always referred to him as my *bolshoi malenki brat* (my big little brother). He missed his wife and daughter and was hopeful they would be able to join him at some point. I took a picture of Nina to bring back to him.

Several of the women from the Center took me on a tour of the incredible Tretyakov Gallery in Moscow, and as we walked on the streets nearby, we came upon McDonald's, which had been opened only a few months previously. This was the time of Mikhail Gorbachev, perestroika and glasnost, a time of greater freedom and openness, and the opening of the first McDonald's restaurant in the Soviet Union was a major event. The lines were about four blocks long, and a Big Mac cost the equivalent of a worker's one week salary. While my companions looked longingly at the restaurant, we needed to get back to the Center for the next planned activities.

Kristina had arranged tickets, and that evening Vadim took me to a concert. We had had only minimal time to talk privately during this trip, and our conversation about his plans for coming to the United States occurred in the lobby of the theater, as the people were leaving the building at the end of the concert and the lights were being turned off.

The next day, several of us did more sightseeing, and then we waited in the parking lot outside another institute to meet up with institute director Anatoly Tkachev from Archangelsk, who had just arrived in Moscow from another city. The arrangement was for me to travel that evening with Anatoly on the overnight train to Archangelsk and stay there for several days to visit his institute. At the train station, Anatoly told me that he was buying a (much cheaper) domestic ticket for me, and that I was not to say anything so the train personnel wouldn't know I was a foreigner. I questioned whether we could get away with this, since I had a Jansport backpack and was wearing sneakers! He said that he had a pin on his lapel showing that he was a member of the Archangelsk City Council, and that should be enough to get me on. He brought along a packet of food to last for the trip.

The train was very clean, and we had our own compartment. The ever-present *provodnitsa* (attendant/tea lady) at the end of the car manned (almost guarded) a huge samovar from which we were able to get tea. Both the conductor checking tickets and the *provodnitsa* gave me strange looks, but neither said anything. Along the way, the train passed a small village.

Looking out the window, I saw a group of small houses, a dirt road and a man standing next to a horse and cart. He was dressed in a black jacket, large flat-top hat and high rubber boots. The entire scene looked like something straight out of *Fiddler on the Roof!*

There were certain times during the trip when the conductor came through the carriage and told Anatoly to close the window shades. I presume this was because we were traveling past some restricted areas. When we got to Archangelsk, Anatoly's driver picked us up and I was dropped off at a very modern hotel. Archangelsk is located well above the Arctic Circle on the Northern Dvina River close to the White Sea; the city is quite close to a major submarine base on the White Sea.

That afternoon, Anatoly took me to his Institute of Ecological Problems of the North, and I was welcomed by a huge bust of Lenin in the lobby and a large portrait of Lenin in Anatoly's office. The staff described some of their ongoing research in this time period, only five years after the Chernobyl disaster. The group was conducting studies on rodents and other wildlife in areas of the North to examine the extent of wildlife contamination due to radiation from the Chernobyl explosion. They also collaborated with researchers in Trömso, Norway; the latter also were studying the same topic. Anatoly told me about one visit to Trömso that ended in a blizzard, requiring him to sleep at the Trömso airport for almost two weeks! This truly is the North.

Anatoly's wife and mother-in-law, who lived with them, seemed very excited to meet me, and we had an enjoyable dinner together at their well-furnished apartment, with Anatoly doing the translating. The next day, we drove to their *dacha* (country house) and had a pleasant and relaxed day with their son and his family. It seemed as if I went 100 years back in time, watching their son brew tea over a large standing coal-fired samovar. There were some very small old wooden churches of medieval design in the area we drove past, which added to the experience.

Beliye Nochi or White Nights, the summer solstice, occurred during this visit. Irina, a woman from Anatoly's institute, took me for a midnight walk through the center of the city. There were many people strolling along this large boulevard and savoring the pleasant weather and the light. A woman walking toward us spotted me and came over and handed me a flower; I obviously was dressed like a foreigner, and it was such a nice gesture. It was very difficult to sleep as it was 24-hour daylight, and I remember waking up to a beautiful blue sky and bright sunshine, looking at the clock and seeing that it was only 3 a.m.

According to plan, Irina accompanied me the next evening on the train back to Moscow, so after a bit of a flurry of activity for food and arrangements we were off. As we got close to Moscow and started to get our things together, the train suddenly stopped. No one knew what was happening, and there was no information from the conductor. Passengers started to get off the train, stand around and stare, and after about twenty minutes or so they slowly started walking along the side of the tracks with their belongings in tow. We began walking as well, as we were totally in the middle of nowhere on a train track. Then suddenly the train very slowly started moving again, and everyone had to run and jump back on the train.

When the train actually pulled into the station in Moscow, Vasili and Lena, a psychologist at the Center, were practically in hysterics. They said there was no information given at the station as to why there was this fairly long delay and where the train was, and they certainly did not want to lose their foreign guest. Fortunately, I learned years ago from my many river-rafting trips in the Grand Canyon that you just "go with the flow," so I was not disturbed at all by this train adventure. I also kept telling everyone my slightly ungrammatical motto, *zhizn bolshoi priklyucheniye!* (Life is a big adventure!)

The next day in Moscow, the major task was to go to a certain office, purchase my plane ticket to Magadan and visit the last of the three institutes that studied the Bering Bridge expedition team. Lena and Natalya, also a psychologist at the Center, accompanied me. Natalya was quite a large woman and the daughter of a Ukrainian general. There was the usual heavy traffic on the street we had to cross, and Natalya protectively grabbed me around my shoulders and pressed me to her ample bosom. So as we crossed the street, I was walking in part leaning to the side, trying to match Natalya's stride. Vasili met us near the office and waited outside.

The office was extremely crowded, but Lena said something to the ticket agent, and we were served right away. I paid for the ticket with my credit card; neither Lena nor Natalya had ever seen a credit card used before, and they were amazed—"Is that all? That's all you have to do? It's so easy"—after the agent ran my card. On the way out, Lena confided that she had told the agent that I was foreign and not used to the smells in the crowded office, so it was important to wait on me right away and not take a chance of me fainting! Outside of the office and meeting up again with Vasili, we all had a good laugh.

Back at the Center, at the end of the work day several of us gathered around a table in a small office. This was the Russian equivalent of Happy Hour. A bottle of high-quality Armenian cognac was passed around. At some point, a man walked slowly by and peered into the room. Vadim quickly put the bottle under the table. This man was the KGB officer stationed in the Center.

Vadim phoned Asilbek Aidareleyev, the institute director in Magadan, several times the next day, concerned whether all of the arrangements for my trip to Magadan were in place. Vadim organized a dinner early that evening at a restaurant on the outskirts of Moscow, attended by about six or seven people from the Center. Since I did not eat meat or poultry at that time, the dilemma was solved by serving me huge portions of the incredibly delicious black caviar from the Caspian Sea. I truly was being pampered big time! The meal at the restaurant lasted for a long time, with lots of good food, laughter and hugs at parting. It really was a memorable occasion.

The following day, a Center driver, along with Vasili and Lena, took me to the airport. As we got closer to Sheremetyevo, there was a large traffic jam and police and other cars were all over the road. When we neared the scene of activity, we saw a smashed car with an open top and two people inside leaning against each other, obviously dead by the extreme pallor of their skin. Once inside the airport, we walked past people seated on benches and then past a man totally passed out, lying across a bench. There was a smashed bottle with glass shards and spilled liquor on the floor all around him. People averted their eyes and just ignored the scene. Walking still farther, we came to a closed area where foreign visitors had to wait for their flights, and local people were restricted from entering. With great concern reflected on their faces, Vasili and Lena said goodbye to me. Lena gave me a bag of food that contained bread and lots of caviar left over from the previous evening for the eight-hour flight to Magadan.

There were no loudspeaker announcements about departing flights. Instead, an airport employee came into the area where I was waiting and listed off several cities including Magadan and Baku; then the entire group in the waiting area was ushered onto a bus. It was rather with a feeling of trepidation that I got on the bus, concerned that I would actually end up in Baku in Azerbaijan and not in Magadan in Siberia! As I walked onto the waiting bus, I kept repeating, "Magadan, Magadan." The bus raced across the tarmac and stopped next to different airplanes. Again, I said "Magadan, Magadan" to the flight attendant to confirm that I actually had walked up the stairway onto the correct plane because she was not checking tickets, but all she did was stare at me.

There were many passengers already seated on the plane; we, the foreigners, were the last to board. I saw an empty middle seat that I walked toward; however, the woman sitting in the aisle seat in that row said something in Russian to me that obviously meant that she did not want me to sit there. The flight attendant now actually moved and came over, and said something to this passenger. I then duly squeezed into the middle seat for this long flight across eight time zones. As we flew through the night, I noticed there were large areas with lights in concentric circles that we were passing, and I saw this pattern more frequently as we got closer to our destination. I later found out that I was seeing prison labor camps; the plane had been flying over the major gulag region of the Soviet Union. Oh!!

Upon arrival in Magadan, institute director Asilbek and his driver were waiting for me. As we left the airport, I saw a large guard tower directly across from the airport grounds, presumably overlooking a prison complex. Magadan is a port city in the Russian Far East located on the Sea of Okhotsk, and it was the epicenter of forced labor camps in Siberia. A major portion of the city population are descendants of the primarily political prisoners imprisoned there during Stalinist and later times, who survived toiling in the gold and silver mines in the area. After their terms were completed, these now former prisoners were forced to remain in exile in Magadan and never allowed to return to their home cities. However, at the time of my visit, there were several scientific institutes in the city and financial inducements for professionals to work there. (My Russian doctoral advisee at the University of Minnesota was from Magadan. Her father had been imprisoned there many years ago and was not allowed to move from the area until the time when Gorbachev instituted perestroika (restructuring).)

The area around Magadan is incredibly beautiful, and it was quite difficult to reconcile the absolutely horrible and tragic conditions that prisoners endured and died from in the camps, and the natural beauty of the surroundings. It also seemed a disconnect to be in Siberia and yet see a woman in a bikini sunbathing on the very rocky beach.

I had a chance to rest for just a short time at the only hotel in Magadan where I stayed, and then Asilbek picked me up for a personal tour of a history museum in the city. The main thing I remember from this tour is that I was fighting to keep my eyes open and avoid swaying too much, as I tried to be polite and listen to the commentary and translation provided just for me. The museum included some displays about the gulag history of the region. Eventually, Asilbek and I had a small meal somewhere, and then I was driven back to the hotel.

My room was quite comfortable, but the small private bathroom was, shall we say, "interesting." To the left of the sink, there was a flat area of the floor with a drain. The water pipes on the sink were extremely long, and experimenting in my jet-lagged state, I realized that the pipes moved. To take a shower, all I needed to do was swing the pipes outward so they were over the floor adjacent to the sink, then squat down and turn on the water. Another adventure!

The next day, Asilbek picked me up and we went to the Institute of Biological Problems of the North, which Asilbek directed. The building was rather modest and austere, in contrast to the facilities I had visited at other places in the Soviet Union. The scientists at the institute conducted research on the health of the indigenous people in the area and, within their facility, studied exercise physiology topics by means of three or four treadmills located in a large room. There were not many people at the institute during the time I was there because it was summer and most of the staff were on holiday, typically traveling back to somewhere in European Russia.

We had a very nice and relaxed dinner that evening at Asilbek's apartment. I am not sure who cooked the meal. His apartment was small but looked quite comfortable. Afterward, we went to a recital held in the municipal building in the center of the city. As we walked over to the venue, I noted the huge statue of Lenin in the central square, similar to what I had seen in other Soviet cities at that time. The recital by three or four musicians was in a large and rather modest room, with plain wooden floors and folding chairs placed in rows in front of the musicians. The adults and children in the audience were dressed in ordinary clothing, unlike the stylish dress I saw on many concertgoers in European Russia.

My cross-country trip across the Soviet Union ended the following day, and I was back at the small Magadan airport. There was only one plane on the tarmac, and the flight was headed to Anchorage. I got settled in and then discovered that there was a US regulation that the plane had to be certified in some way in Khabarovsk before it would be authorized to fly across the Bering Sea to Alaska. So now I was flying south for several hours to Khabarovsk for about a two-hour delay until I could board the plane again.

Khabarovsk is located on the Amur River on the eastern coast of the Soviet Far East and 30.6 km from the border with China. It is close to the region called the Jewish Autonomous Oblast that Stalin decreed as the "homeland" for the Jewish people. I walked around the area near the airport for a short time and noted that most of the people I saw, many sitting on the sidewalk outside the terminal building, looked Central Asian. The men all wore colorful clothing and skullcaps. Back inside the airport, I showed my ticket to the gate agent; he told me that I was not allowed to take rubles out of the country. I had only a small amount left and I asked the agent whom I should give the money to. He smiled and said, "me," so that is what I did.

Back on the plane, I thought we now were heading across the sea to Alaska, but instead, we returned to Magadan. A young American guy sitting next to me on the plane said this was the routine. He worked for a mining company in the Soviet Far East and was familiar with all of these procedures. As the flight continued, vapor gradually started to seep into the cabin, becoming thicker over time. I asked my seat companion what was happening, and he assured me it was alright, the seals on the window often were not very tight and vapor did come in. This was somewhat interesting, although not entirely reassuring. I relaxed and after a short flight the plane landed in Anchorage, and this incredible experience in the Soviet Union was over. I could not believe how fortunate I was to have been to all of the places I was taken to and how wonderful all of the people were that I hoped to continue to work with.

9

INTERLUDE

A person had to do some planning in order to have a private conversation in the Soviet Union because there were listening devices everywhere. People would take walks in a park where they would not be overheard, or try to find other isolated places to converse. I had noticed Vadim unplugging the phone in his apartment when a conversation became sensitive. His family still was strongly motivated to move to the United States, as was Vadim, although everyone had their own individual motivation.

During the past visit, Vadim and I were able to have only a few private discussions considering the options for the type of professional position he potentially could obtain in the United States. I outlined some ideas related to the possibility of Vadim receiving an academic/scientific or related position. Several months later, with the dissolution of the Soviet Union in December 1991 and the declaration of the independent Russian Federation, greater possibilities for commercial and scientific relationships between Russia and the United States emerged. At a number of American universities, foreign and domestic scientists were employed by the US federal government, but their positions were at public and private universities. I thought it might be possible to work out a similar arrangement for Vadim.

Quite independently, the Occupational Health and Safety Products Division of the 3M Company, with its headquarters in a suburb of St. Paul, Minnesota, expressed an interest in the respirators manufactured in Russia that were used by the cleanup workers following the Chernobyl disaster. Vadim's Center had been involved in the development and testing of personal protective equipment for a number of years, and he had direct experience with these respirators, having monitored worker safety at Chernobyl and other places.

Alex Shevchenko, a Ukrainian-speaking manager at 3M, contacted Vadim and met with him at the Center to examine the Russian respirators and pursue 3M's other Russian business agendas. The 3M Company had an overriding interest in establishing a local connection to set up their own factory in Russia to manufacture 3M respirators and other products. Their plan, as conveyed by Alex, was to bring Vadim to Minnesota for a meeting to work out details regarding these commercial interests. Vadim told Alex about my collaboration with the Center and that I was living in the same Twin Cities area; he asked Alex to coordinate this meeting with me so Vadim and I could continue with some of our own research interests. A meeting was set up, and Vadim arrived in Minnesota together with Anatoly Tkachev from Archangelsk. I was very surprised and delighted to see Anatoly again.

Because of Vadim's continued work with the Russian space program (Roscosmos) on protective equipment and the overall health protection of cosmonauts, I thought this visit was an excellent opportunity to introduce him to some of the NASA researchers I knew. I had been invited to the NASA Ames Research Center (ARC) the year before by psychologist Dr. Mary Connors to give a presentation on my expedition research; I contacted Mary to see whether there was an interest in having Vadim give a presentation at ARC on the psychological support programs Roscosmos was using. She agreed, although this still was a very difficult period in terms of US relationships with Russia, and it took some time to get the security permission for Vadim to enter the ARC complex. Following the 3M meetings, Anatoly remained in Minneapolis with university post-doctoral fellow Misha Arkharov as his companion, and Vadim and I flew to California for the meeting.

The security person who checked Vadim's passport and looked up the entry permission was totally startled to see a Russian in front of her. There had only been two other Russians in total who had ever entered the ARC complex. I was told to be with Vadim at all times, even when he went to the restroom, but that was where I drew the line! His talk went well, and we also toured the excellent ARC bedrest and space suit development facilities. That evening, Mary had us over to her house and we had a fun and relaxed time. She had music and snacks, and we both were totally amused to watch Vadim eating peanuts and dancing! I said to Mary, laughing, "Can you believe this?" She shook her head and said, "No," and we laughed again. Vadim definitely was not the stereotype of the beefy glowering Soviet man.

Vadim and Anatoly returned to Russia, and the negotiations with 3M continued. During this time, I met Dr. Dave Charles from the Armed Forces Radiobiology Research Institute (AFRRI) in Washington, DC, at a psychology conference. I told him about Vadim's work as one of the first medical officers at Chernobyl and his participation at International Atomic Energy Agency (IAEA) meetings in Vienna. About six months later,

Dave arranged for Vadim to give a talk at AFRRI on the Chernobyl health ramifications, and 3M also indicated that they were interested in having Vadim come back for more meetings in St. Paul. Return arrangements were made, and in May 1992 I met Vadim at JFK, and we flew the shuttle flight to Washington. His AFRRI talk was well received, and it was the start of negotiations for Vadim to have a closer involvement with AFRRI.

Back in Minnesota, Vadim had additional discussions with the 3M group, and I introduced him to Professor Ira Glover, the head of the Division of Environmental and Occupational Health (EOH) in the School of Public Health at the University of Minnesota. Vadim's Chernobyl and related experiences were of particular relevance to EOH in regard to their impact on the public health of large-scale populations. The various meetings went well, and Vadim returned to Russia. I privately told both Ira and the AFRRI director about Vadim's interest in immigrating to the United States.

Following numerous discussions, an arrangement was made for Vadim to be awarded a one-year fellowship through AFRRI and centered at EOH as his home base. I mentioned to Ira that Vadim's daughter Marya was working on a PhD analyzing Chernobyl health data and asked whether she might be able to share some office space and use one of the computers in his department. Unexpectedly, he said that he could award her a one-year research fellowship in EOH to continue this research.

Because of the timing of Marya's fellowship, Marya and Vadim's wife Polina arrived in Minnesota at the beginning of September 1992. They were staying temporarily at our house with my husband's help while I flew to Moscow for more meetings focused on MMPI and other research.

10

MOSCOW, KIEV, CHERNOBYL, ST. PETERSBURG, RYAZAN TRIP

September 1992

Vadim and expeditioner Dmitry Shparo coordinated my visit to work on several projects, including initial planning for a Chernobyl study and interviews with the participants of a six-month, 15,000 km wheelchair expedition organized by Dmitry and his *Club Priklyucheniye* (Adventure Club). I also wanted to talk with Vasili and others about the progress on the Russian MMPI-2 translation and plans for the Russian standardization. On my last visit, Kristina told me that her daughter's greatest wish was to have a Barbie doll, so indeed I brought a Barbie doll for her daughter and a game for her younger son.

This period in Russia continued to be one of extreme economic hardship and scarcity; funds to support scientific research were very sparse. The staff at former Soviet Union scientific institutions were very eager to pursue any possibility of being involved in international research. They sought out my help to introduce them to psychological tests they were not familiar with and develop research protocols that followed Western-style methodology. They also were interested in the contacts I could make with scientific and other institutes in the United States potentially to obtain funds to further research in Russia. I was trying my best to further these aims, with the plan of submitting a collaborative Chernobyl research proposal to one of the US Institutes of Health. The unspoken agenda between Vadim and me was that he would serve as a primary investigator from the American side. First, however, we needed to have some pilot data to strengthen any proposal we eventually would submit.

I was housed again at the hotel across the park from the Center, but now with the dissolution of the Soviet Union and some of its restrictions, the atmosphere at the hotel seemed more relaxed. I did not notice a KGB car out front. My first activity at the Center was a requested presentation on my trek in the Himalayas in Nepal, and then meetings with others.

Professor Valentin Gavrilov, director of the Belarus Institute of Physiology and head of the Belarus Academy of Sciences, and his son Dr. Alexei Gavrilov, came to the Center from Minsk, Belarus, to meet with me and others to develop some specific plans for the submission of a Chernobyl grant proposal. A great deal of the research efforts at Valentin's institute was on population health effects of the Chernobyl disaster. Belarus was the region that was the most highly contaminated after the Chernobyl explosion; due to the prevailing winds, the radioactive plume moved in a northwesterly direction, directly over Belarus.

We planned for a small pilot study of two villages in Belarus, one village that government radiation monitoring indicated had suffered significant contamination and a second village that had not been contaminated, that is, was "clean." We were particularly interested in a phenomenon the Russian psychologists termed "radiophobia," a fear of having been contaminated by radiation and then attributing all physical and/or emotional problems to this presumed exposure. I suggested we develop a questionnaire to evaluate this phenomenon, and we discussed specific topics to cover in the items we developed. The plan was to examine whether there were differences in health attitudes and health behaviors between the contaminated and non-contaminated village groups, studying both adults and adolescents who were too young to remember the actual explosion. We agreed that I would write questionnaire items when I returned home and send the draft to Valentin and Alexei for their inputs. After modifications, Alexei would then translate the questionnaire that we would use for our project.

Alexei took charge of the data collection in Belarus. We planned to use the pilot study findings as a rationale for a large grant proposal that I would write and submit to a US funding agency. We also planned, with the Moscow Center group, to include in the proposal or as a separate proposal funds for the aggregation of the annual physical health data collected by the Scientific Centers of Radiation Medicine in Moscow, Minsk and Kiev. During the era of the Soviet Union, all of these centers had been under the centralized control of the Institute of Biophysics in Moscow. Currently, the centers operated independently, and each country had to secure its own funding.

Vasili and I visited the Scientific Center of Radiation Medicine in Moscow, and I was shown an extremely comprehensive computerized population health database, spanning the period from the time of the explosion to the present. During the period of my visit, the annual health evaluations in each of the countries affected by radiation continued, although they were no longer coordinated from Moscow.

The psychologists associated with the Russian MMPI-2 translation at the Moscow Center gave me an update on their progress. Vasili in turn was making initial inquiries with different groups to provide normative data once the translation was completed and accepted. Kristina and the other Center translators' efforts were highly important for the success of the project, and considering their excellent expertise in the English language, I was comfortable that we would have a valid translation. Upon completion, the next step was for the University of Minnesota's language institute to evaluate the translation and provide feedback to the University of Minnesota Press, which held the copyright on the measure.

Vasili took me to visit the noted Professor Angelina Guscova at Hospital Number 6 in Moscow. All professionals entering a hospital are required to wear a white coat; I was handed a rather aromatic one, hanging on a hook by the entrance to the building. Dr. Guscova was the leading authority in the country on acute radiation sickness. The hospital served as the centralized center for the entire Soviet Union for treating patients affected by radiation and other forms of contamination; 134 patients who developed acute radiation sickness after Chernobyl were treated there under her supervision.

Dr. Guscova was an absolutely warm and charming person, and she described the treatment procedures that had been carried out on the Chernobyl firefighters and other patients. I really was in awe in her presence, knowing her accomplishments and the esteem she was held by my Russian colleagues. Vadim's daughter Marya had worked at this hospital, and Dr. Guscova knew that Marya was already in Minnesota to begin her fellowship. She told me that she was very pleased that Marya had this opportunity.

Vasili arranged for me to visit a hospital that treated patients with eating disorders. I had asked for this opportunity because of my own long-standing research in this area, and I was interested in the treatment approaches used in Russia. At the hospital, we met with Professor Tsyvilko and an associate, both in the Department of Psychiatry and Medical Psychology, People's Friendship University (named after Patrice Lumumba). We conversed for a while about our respective interests, and then an aide escorted into the room a teenaged female patient with anorexia nervosa, who described her symptoms and the treatment she was receiving. I was intrigued by the fact of the universality of the psychological attitudes and behaviors related to the progression of her illness, and heard, in her own words (translated), her progress in treatment. I suggested to the physicians that they write a paper in English describing their treatment philosophy and methods, which were different in many ways from some of the more usual Western approaches. I would then polish their text for submission to a treatment-oriented journal. We subsequently worked together, and the paper was published in an international eating disorders journal.

On the way back to the Center, we stopped outside of the main complex of what all referred to as Patrice Lumumba University, founded in 1960 to help students from developing nations receive a professional education. I was quite impressed with the large number of students from countries in Africa whom I saw walking across the campus grounds.

My next visit was to Chernobyl. With all of my disaster and expedition research, it is incredibly helpful if I am able to visit the area where the events took place. In my view, there is no substitute for actually experiencing at least the environment where the activities occurred to gain greater insight into the psychological impact of the experience for the group I am studying.

I was accompanied to Chernobyl by my "team." Vasili, Kristina and I traveled by train to Kiev, a distance of about 755 km. Kiev in turn is approximately 95 km from Chernobyl. Vasili now owned and brought along a Panasonic video camera that he was able to buy in part through MMPI funds. (Sometimes one needed to be resourceful to buy things that were not readily available in Russia and were quite expensive if they were available. Professor James (Jim) Butcher in my department was the leading authority on MMPI and a co-investigator on the development of MMPI-2. There was an MMPI meeting in Belgium that Vasili received permission from the Center to attend. The University of Minnesota Press, through Jim, provided Vasili with some funds to help with meeting expenses, which he received when he got to Belgium. Vasili was able to save some of this expense money and, voila!, he bought a Panasonic video camera which he dearly loved, and he recorded our entire trip.)

The train ride was very comfortable and fun. I had on jeans and a sweater and the others also wore casual clothing. I enjoyed looking at the changing landscape and the people that I caught glimpses of in the villages and towns along the way. We had a compartment to ourselves, and my companions produced several large bags with an array of food, soft drinks and a bottle of Armenian cognac for lunch. There was a small tray adjacent to the window that pulled out, and that was our table.

We were met at the Kiev train station by Dr. Dimitry Bondarenko, Scientific Leader of the Institute of Clinical Radiology of Ukraine,

Scientific Center of Radiation Medicine, who drove us to an apartment with beautiful furnishings that was specially reserved for visiting scientists. We each had our own room and got settled in very quickly. There was food in the refrigerator, and we had dinner in the apartment. The next morning, Vasili went out to get some food for our breakfast, and he even scouted for open kiosks to find some Pepsi Cola, which he knew I liked. (I certainly was being pampered, although this was not my style or expectation.)

We took the train to Chernobyl and were met there by the health scientists who worked at a small center on the outskirts of the village of Chernobyl. They had prepared a lavish lunch for us, and they shared their concern about not having enough funds to maintain their health monitoring of the workers and other staff, as the power plant was still in operation. I described our long-term plans through the Center and Belarus to submit a research proposal to a US agency. They were very eager for me to contact different agencies in terms of their own funding needs. I promised to do so, and I followed up on their request when I returned home.

Over all of my visits, I felt a tremendous responsibility to be successful in any proposal that ultimately I would be responsible for submitting. I wanted to be of as much help as I could to all of these excellent and dedicated people, many of whom were good friends. I explained to everyone how the proposal evaluation system worked in the United States. I stated that I could not guarantee funding, but certainly I would try as hard as I could to be successful; also, that I would enlist the help of other scientists at the University of Minnesota and elsewhere on all proposals.

The small village of Chernobyl was quite picturesque. There were small wooden houses with traditional Ukrainian designs spread out across grassy areas; however, I saw that a number of the houses had a sign on them that, when translated, read "people live here." After the explosion, the population from this area (the 30 km exclusion zone) was evacuated and moved to apartments in large building blocks in Kiev. However, the Soviet authorities allowed older people who wanted to return to their homes, irrespective of radiation danger, to do so. The attitude of these older residents was that this place was their home which had been in their family for many generations, and if there was a danger of getting cancer twenty years in the future, they were not worried about that.

After our lunch and conversation, a driver along with a guide from the Chernobyl center drove us past the Chernobyl checkpoint up to a large fenced area with a gate; the four-building power plant complex was on the other side! It was an incredibly awesome experience, and also a bit anxiety-provoking, to actually see the damaged reactor at some distance in front of me—not on a photo or a video. The car that we drove in up to the fence was "clean," meaning it was relatively free of radioactive contamination. Now we needed to walk through the gate to a different car waiting within the complex on the other side of the fence, to take us closer to the plant. Our guide produced a hand-held dosimeter; the numbers showed that the car was "dirty." There was some contamination on the car as well as in the atmosphere.

Kristina decided to wait for us in the clean car, saying that she had small children and wanted to be sure she was safe. As Vasili, the guide and I stood within the complex, a large bus drove past carrying plant workers donned in white smocks and hats, who had just finished their work shift. Vasili and I went into a metal siding building, walked through a scanner and then donned protective clothing that was stacked in bins in the room—a very thick jacket, pants, a hat that fit all the way down past the ears and looked like a chef's hat, heavy boots and gloves. The driver and guide were waiting for us on the other side of the building in this different car; their attitude was that they were macho and did not need protective clothing. Next, we drove up near another fence closer to the destroyed reactor and got out of the car. The dosimeter our guide was holding was giving off constant and more rapid readings as we walked along, and we were careful not to get too close to this fence.

Now, the destroyed fourth building with the sarcophagus enclosing the roof and the entire building was looming close in front of us. I visualized what the situation would have been like at the time of the explosion and the aftermath. Vadim had the responsibility of supervising the safety of the cleanup workers ("liquidators"), who had to climb a ladder to the top of the adjacent building, run across the roof with a shovel in hand to scoop up radioactive debris from the roof, dispose of it and run back down the ladder, all in a little over 2 minutes. In this 2-minute time frame, a worker would have been exposed to his lifetime health limit of radiation.

There were large pits in the vicinity of the reactors that were dug during the cleanup phase; many vehicles and other large pieces of equipment are permanently buried there because they were too large to adequately decontaminate. Therefore, even though the pits are covered over, this permanent presence will have an effect on the environment for hundreds of years, if not longer.

We returned to the car and drove back to the same metal siding building where we deposited our protective gear and passed through the scanner. As I walked out of the building, I looked at this large fence several hundred meters in front of us, separating the "bad" from the "good," in terms of radioactivity. We drove up to the fence, walked through the gate and did the exchange from the dirty car to the clean car, where Kristina was waiting for us.

Our next stop was Pripyat, the town where fifty thousand plant workers, scientists and their families had lived. As we were driving, I gazed at a surreal landscape that at this point in time was six years after the disaster. I was struck by the peculiar color of the grass and trees I saw along the way. The trees and intact leaves on the branches as well as the grass all had a weird brownish/gold color that was caused by the radiation that was released by the explosion and radioactive fire. Although wind gusts still circulated contaminated dust and debris from the trees, the amount of radiation circulated by the wind was relatively small.

Pripyat is within the 30 km "exclusion zone" and is completely evacuated. In the immediate aftermath of the explosion, the information about the extent of the damage and the levels of radiation released was extremely confused. Government authorities were in denial and at first tried to minimize the extent of the disaster. However, some school children were given iodine pills to block radioactive iodine from being absorbed by the thyroid gland even before the evacuation occurred. The evacuation order was not made until a day and a half after the explosion; residents were given only 50 minutes notice to leave. They were told that the evacuation was only temporary; buses and trucks took them to shelter in Kiev.

The official government denial continued, and the general population was not informed about the dire seriousness of the disaster. Although government officials evacuated their own families from the area, a bicycle marathon, kicking up radioactive dust, was held in Kiev that weekend.

The experience walking the streets of Pripyat also was totally surreal. The typical large Soviet-style concrete-block apartment buildings were still standing. Given the generally poor maintenance of buildings that I had observed in the Soviet Union, the signs of deterioration did not seem unusual—the buildings looked like they still could be inhabited. We walked past a very large sports hall, administrative buildings, stores and other facilities that would be typical of a small Soviet city.

But it was a ghost town. There was grass growing in the cracks on the sidewalk, and, looking into a building, the silent equipment and deserted objects lying on the floor added to an otherworldly feeling. To add to the total weirdness of the experience, I heard music constantly playing that sounded like a funeral dirge. Vasili said that someone had put a loudspeaker on top of one of the buildings, and indeed, it was some type of melancholic music that was being played continuously. Another example of the dramatic Russian *dusha* (soul). We rather silently walked back to our waiting car, each of us, I think, lost in our thoughts of what we had just experienced over the last few hours.

When we returned to the Chernobyl center, a driver was waiting to take us directly to the Ukrainian National Chernobyl Museum in Kiev. The museum commemorates the 28 first-response firefighters who died of acute radiation sickness within weeks of the explosion and the additional firefighters and plant workers who died at later times. There were photos of the deceased firefighters, displays of jackets, helmets and other equipment. The centerpiece of the museum is a large diorama showing the progression of the so-called safety-check procedures at the plant that caused the explosion and then the movement of the first-response firefighters from Kiev to the fourth building explosion site. There also are media depictions of the environmental and cultural ramifications of the disaster.

That evening, we again had dinner at the apartment. Food had somehow materialized and a friend of Vasili's joined us, arriving with some additional food and a small bottle of vodka. We spent a long time in conversation at the dinner table, and in the tradition that I quickly learned to appreciate, we proposed a few toasts to each other.

The next day we had time for sightseeing. We toured the famous and beautiful Lavra monastery in Kiev, known as the monastery of the caves, and walked through its complex of catacombs. We also stood at a vantage point outside the monastery and simply enjoyed the view of the Dnieper River flowing nearby. We were accompanied for part of our visit that day by Dimitry, director of the Ukrainian radiation scientific center, and his wife.

At my request, we also went to Babi Yar, a large ravine near Kiev in which close to thirty-four thousand Jewish men, women and children were massacred in 1941 over a one-week period by German forces, with the help of the Ukrainian police. There is an outstanding, dramatic large monument alongside the ravine, and it was an absolutely devastating experience to view this site and know what had transpired there. (I recently found out from a cousin who did some genealogy research that I likely had two maternal great-uncles who were murdered at Babi Yar.)

Back in Kiev, we stopped at an active Jewish synagogue. There were many people in the courtyard because it was the eve of Rosh Hashanah, the Jewish New Year. I walked around the courtyard and was struck by how much these older men and women looked like they could have been my own relatives. I was able to communicate with some of the people, speaking to them in very basic Yiddish. It was a very warm and emotional experience following the visit to Babi Yar. The people I spoke with said they were getting some financial support and goods through the American Joint Jewish Distribution Committee located in New York; most of their surviving relatives had emigrated to Israel.

We had dinner, and in the late evening we were taken to the Kiev airport for our flight to St. Petersburg. The plan was to visit a hospital that had a hyperbaric chamber in which they were treating patients with different types of health problems. We also were scheduled to visit another facility, but at that point, no one seemed to know what institute or what was on the agenda. Oh well ... go with the flow!

Upon arrival at the airport, we were told that there was a flight delay, and we spent several hours waiting in the terminal. Finally, all passengers on the flight were led out a door and told to wait outside the terminal building. It was quite dark and a bit eerie, and we waited for a long time. Finally, a man slowly walked back from the vicinity of the plane, giving all those waiting a rather quizzical look as he passed, like "What are you doing here?" He was carrying a jar about one quarter full with a substance that looked like grease. We then were given the okay to board the plane. It was now about one o'clock in the morning, and we kept our trust in Aeroflot!

A number of people of Central Asian origin boarded the plane carrying cardboard boxes, which they placed in the middle of the aisle—rather dangerous if there needed to be an emergency evacuation. But none of the flight attendants said anything, so that was how we flew to St. Petersburg. Kristina sat in the seat next to me, and while I had an intact seat belt, her seat only had one half of the belt. I did not feel comfortable being strapped in while she was not able to, so I did not use my seat belt. When the plane started to descend, one of the men with the boxes stood up on crutches and remained standing for the rest of the time until the plane landed in St. Petersburg. Again, none of the attendants said anything, and that was how we landed.

It now was about five o'clock in the morning, and a driver and scientist from a disaster satellite center in St. Petersburg were wearily waiting to meet us and take us to our hotel. There was a glitch in the room arrangements, but Kristina and I were very comfortable to share a room. It seemed that we barely got to sleep when there was a knock on the door; the same woman from the St. Petersburg center was waiting to take us to our first appointment, the hospital. A group of about six people was waiting as we were ushered into a conference room and introductions were made. Then instead of tea, one of the women placed small glasses all around that were filled with cognac! Not exactly what we needed at that moment. I did take a few sips out of politeness, but I did not want to take a chance of falling asleep in the middle of a welcoming toast.

We were briefed on the activities of the hospital. The director was very keen to tell us about the very positive results they were obtaining treating patients with a range of disorders in their bariatric chamber. We toured the hospital and were introduced to an American couple who had heard about the bariatric treatment the hospital group was using to improve hearing in deaf patients. They had brought their 6–year-old boy who was deaf to the hospital for evaluation and treatment. We met the little boy, referred to as the *malchik*, and had a chance to talk with him. He could hear us quite well. The staff showed us data they had collected on his auditory acuity, and according to the staff and the parents, there was a marked improvement in his hearing. The staff was very eager to disseminate this information in the United States and other countries.

Following this visit, we again squeezed into a small Lada, and now we were driving across the city. I had no idea where we were going. At one point, semi-humorously, I whispered to Kristina sitting next to me, "Kristina, where are they taking us?" She didn't know either. We both collapsed in giggles and found out that our next stop was at what was termed a "diving institute." We were met by a psychologist at the facility, who, we realized very quickly by his loud voice, probably was hard of hearing. We talked a bit, and then he took us to a room that had a large iron safe about 3.5 m tall with a padlock on it. He opened the safe and took out some papers, which he placed on a table.

All this time, Vasili was filming us with his video camera. He had zoomed in on the cover sheet that had a large stamp on it. I presume the stamp indicated some level of classified material. Now, the psychologist stood on one side of me talking very loudly in my left ear, while Kristina stood on the other side, translating into my right ear. This was not a great experience after so little sleep the night before. The psychologist was showing me cognitive and other psychological test data, indicating normal functioning on these tests. Only later I realized that the tests probably had been conducted on personnel deployed on nuclear submarines.

We then were ushered into a conference room for a chat with the director of the institute and his deputy. It was when I saw the photos on the wall of very large submarines and aircraft carriers that I was able to put two and two together about the data I had just seen. In the course of the discussion, I really did not see any possibility for a research collaboration.

Our plan was to have dinner in the room that Kristina and I shared, and Vasili went out to buy food. There was no refrigerator in the room, so according to tradition, the leftover food was placed on the outside window sill to finish up for breakfast. Later that evening, the woman who had met us that morning for the hospital visit came over to our room to talk with Vasili. Their center was extremely needful of funds, and she was hopeful Vasili would talk with Vadim to try to obtain more funds for their activities.

The next day was planned for sightseeing in this beautiful city of palaces and museums, accompanied for some of the time by the same woman from the St. Petersburg center. Before leaving the hotel for the day, Vasili asked me if I wanted to see another nuclear power plant. Kristina, who always was so quiet and polite, immediately burst out, "Oh no!" I said as well in a quieter voice that as long as we were in St. Petersburg, I wanted to take at least a little time to visit the famed Hermitage museum. That morning, we toured two spectacular palaces and surrounding grounds, and walked over to view the Pushkin monument. Vasili happily videotaped everything we saw.

At the entrance to each palace, an ever-present babushka was seated taking tickets, all the while sending grim looks in our direction. The overwhelming amount of gold, silver, gilt and paintings were impressive, but it certainly brought to mind the tremendous contrast between the splendor of these palaces and the living conditions of the peasants and others that fomented the Russian Revolution.

Because our time was short and we were scheduled to take the night train back to Moscow, we skipped lunch and went straight to the Hermitage. Afterward, at about six in the evening, we walked around the streets looking for somewhere to eat. The restaurants we saw were still closed for the dinner hour, but we did find one café that was open. The waitress who was quite a large woman came over to our table, placed her hands on her hips, looked down on us and in a surly voice said, "Why are you eating here? The food is terrible. You should go across the street!" Vasili patiently explained that nothing else was open, and she begrudgingly handed us the rather limited menu. (The concept of service and certainly tips had not as yet arrived in Russia, apparently.)

We ordered our meal and eventually she brought our food along with some kind of nondescript juice that we couldn't identify. When Vasili rather derisively asked her later for seconds on "that juice," she again stood upright and said, "That is not juice—it's punch." Whatever! And she was right: the food was really bad, but we were hungry, it didn't matter and we laughed alot. We later walked to the train station for the trip back to Moscow. Kristina and I shared a compartment with pulldown beds. Vasili's ticket placed him in another compartment with an unknown woman. She was not happy that Vasili was there, and he came to visit us a few times before going back to his compartment to get some sleep. Otherwise, it was an uneventful trip.

In the morning, a driver met us at our train and took us back to the Center. There was a van waiting for me in the Center parking lot; Sasha Tenyakshev, Dmitry's right-hand man and Bering Bridge expedition participant, and a film crew were there. The plan was to drive directly to the town of Ryazan to meet up with the disabled members and the support staff of the wheelchair expedition team that Dmitry organized. The team was spending a day or two outside of a children's hospital on the outskirts of Ryazan for rest and resupply. I went into the Center for a brief moment and then Lena and a few others came out "to see this amazing lady," as I prepared to stretch out across the back bench of the van to get more sleep on the way to Ryazan. The city is about 180 km southeast of Moscow and birthplace of famed physiologist Ivan Pavlov.

The wheelchair expedition was Dmitry's idea, and with his fame and hard work through the Adventure Club, he was able to organize and successfully receive support for this endeavor even during quite difficult economic times in Russia. His vision was to demonstrate that even though a person has a severe handicap, it is still possible for them to accomplish great physical feats. Also, this feat would prove to the disabled person that their lives still had meaning. At that time, disabled people were simply expected to stay at home. There were no wheelchairs manufactured or available in Russia; Dmitry obtained the wheelchairs for the expeditioners from Sweden.

The expedition participants were three paraplegic former athlete men, accompanied by four able-bodied escorts. They covered over 15,000 km from Vladivostok on the Pacific coast of the Russian Far East to St. Petersburg in a six-month period. This really was quite an impressive feat—the disabled participants traveled this entire distance in their wheelchairs. During the early part of the expedition, there were no actual roads in many areas; they had to ride on rock-filled dirt trails, often falling out of their wheelchairs at the bottom of a steep hill.

Dmitry, at the start of the expedition planning, asked if I was interested in studying the team, which I was. I wanted to examine team processes and also the relationship between the disabled participants and their able-bodied escorts. Both groups completed a short questionnaire each evening that assessed team effectiveness, the efficiency of communication between groups and the resulting decisions made, food and medical quality, and an exertion rating. My plan for Ryazan was to collect the questionnaires completed at that point in the journey and conduct a semi-structured interview with each of the three wheelchair participants.

We stopped for lunch on the way to Ryazan and eventually arrived at a large sprawling building with wings on each side that looked like it could have been an estate in Czarist times. The concrete on the building walls was crumbling and the place almost looked abandoned. However, there were four personnel carriers parked alongside of the main building and lots of activity with about twelve people going back and forth among these vehicles. Each vehicle had been remodeled for a different function—kitchen, sleeping quarters with bunk beds, massage facility and a medical clinic. The entourage included drivers, cooks, physician, massage therapist and the escort personnel.

We were greeted and ushered into the main building by the hospital director, who then showed us the rooms we would sleep in that night. The director led Sasha and me to a large room with two beds and asked if that room would suffice (Russian customs did not make a distinction by gender in terms of room arrangements). However, Sasha saw my startled expression and said in a low voice to the director, *oden* (alone). So I had this large, although bare and crumbling, room all to myself.

Conducting international collaborative research while relying on email messages has its challenges. I was wondering why I kept getting an increasing number of insistent emails from Dmitry asking me how long I wanted the group to keep doing the daily questionnaire. I kept writing that I wanted them to continue with the protocol until I got to Ryazan to do the interviews. When we arrived in Ryazan, I saw a gigantic pile of boxes and I was told that all of the questionnaires were in the boxes. It turned out that there had been a miscommunication and Dmitry understood that the entire expedition entourage, including drivers, cooks, and so forth were supposed to do the questionnaires each evening! I dispensed the entire group from doing any more questionnaires and filled a carry-on bag with the data from the three wheelchair and four escort participants. (Along with the film documentary of the expedition, Dmitry wrote a book in which he included a translation of every one of my emails to him about the research!)

We ate dinner seated at a table with the director and the expeditioners; later, our two film crew members set up their equipment to film some of the activities, including my interviews. It was still later in the evening when I began the first interview with Sasha serving as my interpreter. These interviews turned out to be quite emotional; each participant described what their lives were like before and after their accident, how they were coping with their disability and the psychological meaning of the expedition for each of them.

The major themes conveyed by the participants were the lack of interest by the community and their feelings that their lives had lost meaning. The 26-year-old youngest participant, in an extremely anguished voice and expression, said, "How come a professor has to come all the way from America and take an interest in us, when no one in Russia even cares?" Now with my psychology therapist rather than research hat on, I tried to reassure him that his life did have meaning; with expeditions such as they were doing to promote public awareness, their individual lives were important. I recall a total hush in the room by the film crew, people practically holding their breath as I had this incredibly emotional conversation, through Sasha's words.

The questionnaire component of the study assessed relationships between the able-bodied leader and staff and the disabled participants. Our findings indicated that clear communication of the daily schedule by the leader was significantly related to feelings of friendliness among all of the group members and high ratings of the fairness and quality of other person's decisions. Perceived exertion by the wheelchair participants was negatively related to views of the adequacy of decision processes. These findings highlight the importance of decisions made by the able-bodied leader on the social climate of the group and also the influence of these decisions on feelings of exertion or stamina by the disabled participants during the daily wheelchair trek.

The next morning, we were taken on a tour of the children's hospital that housed perhaps one hundred children and adolescents. We walked into a large room where some children were smiling and waving at us from their beds that had iron railings around them. There also were several classrooms, a large meeting space and many empty rooms in the building. I noted a large number of able-bodied children and teenaged boys and girls in various rooms; I wondered whether the facility also was an orphanage and/or a place for children with behavior problems.

After the tour, the entire hospital staff and occupants gathered for a ceremony for the expeditioners. The three men were seated in their wheelchairs in a row facing the audience; a boy about 10 years old in a wheelchair was wheeled over to flank one side of the row. I was asked to sit with the group at the other end of the row. The staff presented each of the men a large bouquet of flowers and there were speeches by the director and others. After saying goodbye to everyone, we headed back to Moscow, questionnaires in tow, stopping along the way to buy strings of garlic from a woman standing by the highway. I met up with Dmitry at a later time in Moscow.

The room in the Moscow hotel close to the Center I was staying at had phones in the room, and one evening I wanted to place a call home. The phone did not seem to be working; I went down to the desk and in my very limited Russian tried to explain the situation. For some reason, I kept saying "area code, area code" in my best Russian accent. Actually, I was trying to find out the international phone code from Russia to the United States to make a call. The woman at the desk signaled for a man to come up to the room with me—it may have been the *militzia* (policeman). He checked the dialing device and said all was fine. When I later tried again to make a call, nothing happened. I mentioned this to Lena the next morning at the Center, and she looked at me very amused and said, "Gloria, you really didn't expect to make a call to the United States from that hotel, did you?" Even with perestroika, some things did not change.

Another evening at the hotel, I was getting ready for bed when suddenly I heard from a nearby room the sounds of a woman screaming. The screams continued for what seemed like a long time, and I opened my door and warily looked out to see what was happening. People from other rooms were doing the same, but no one went over to the room where the screams were coming from to do anything about it. I sorely wanted to call the desk and tell them what was happening, but my Russian skills were not good enough to explain the situation. Eventually the screams stopped.

The last formal event that I was involved in on this visit was a disaster conference attended by high-level civilian and military professionals from Russia and former Soviet Block countries. Vadim was extremely busy during the time I was in Moscow, and he asked if I would accompany him to this conference, which he had a major role in. He also was very busy on the morning of the event, and it was quite late by the time we left the Center for the conference. He had his driver put a blue emergency light on the vehicle, and we sped across major traffic, car horn beeping, to get to the conference site. The Minister of Health and many other dignitaries were waiting for him to arrive to begin the proceedings. Vadim gave the opening presentation, and the next few hours passed with other presentations on disaster medicine topics.

Following the presentations, there was a VIP banquet that included the international visitors. Vadim sat on my right, and a very tall Russian two-star general was seated on my left. The general's English skills were good, and we made some small talk. As the meal progressed, the cognac was flowing (vodka was still hard to obtain during this period) and the toasts got longer and longer. The protocol was that a person stood up and gave a toast and then all of the people in the room quickly stood up, held their glasses out and downed their drink in one gulp. I quickly realized this was not a good thing for me to do, and I only sipped a small amount of liquor after each toast. At one point, someone gave a very lengthy toast and Vadim urged me not to stand up. (A general toast to Communism – who knows?)

There was a man sitting directly across from me at this large table who did not look Russian. After the banquet had been going on for a few hours, he got up and offered a very long toast. I duly stood up with the others, but this tall general looked down on me and asked if I understood that this was a toast to Cuba and the Red army! This still was a time of tense relations between the United States and Russia, exacerbated by the Cuban missile crisis. At this point, after so many toasts, even drinking a small amount each time, all I could say was *druzhba, druzhba* (friendship), and I stood for the toast.

Eventually, we had to get back to the Center. The psychologists were waiting for us to do some final planning for the MMPI-2 research. We came rushing back into the building, Vadim apologizing for the delay and on my part trying to focus again on research. Marc, the psychologist who on an earlier visit was incensed that I had been given the Chernobyl power plant MMPI data to analyze, again was rather abrasive. He had a difference of opinion on the wording of some of the instructions and insisted on making some changes that I did not agree with. Our discussion became quite heated, fueled in part by the number of toasts I drank at the banquet. The others in the group resolved the issue according to my satisfaction, and everyone went home.

Vadim had a small gathering in his apartment that evening. Some of the people who came over were from the Center; also present was Dr. Vladislav Brabec, his close colleague from the Czech Republic. Vladislav was the director of the Czech Labor Medicine Institute, an institute that specialized in the health monitoring of people exposed to environmental contamination. Although there was a great deal of camaraderie that evening, as Vladislav was leaving, he whispered to me that he did not think that Vadim was going to live very long because of the large amount of radiation he had been exposed to at Chernobyl. He then gave me a hug and departed.

It was now the weekend, and Vasili and I drove with Vadim to Vadim's dacha outside of Moscow. Following a centralized collective structure, the other dachas in the area were owned by members of the Center and those working in related areas. It was extremely nice to get out to the countryside to relax after the very intensive schedule I had been on, together with my ever-friendly escort Vasili. Vadim was very proud of the vegetables and flowers that were growing in his yard, and we laughed a lot as he picked large ripe cucumbers, which we called Chernobyl cucumbers.

Some of their friends came over, and I told them that Vasili was trying to teach me an important skill that he said was part of the training of a Russian military officer. It consisted of holding your arm and hand straight out, placing a shot of vodka on the back of your hand, slowly bending and raising your arm until you could trap the glass with your lips, then moving your head back and downing the shot. Actually, I never did learn how to do this.

I returned to the United States to focus on contacting administrators from relevant US government funding agencies, to ascertain which agency would have the most interest in evaluating a large-scale project on the Chernobyl population. If successful, Vadim and I would co-lead this research that would have a particular emphasis on mental health factors. Seven weeks later, Vadim arrived in Minnesota and his new life in America began.

11
INTERLUDE

Vadim and I worked together to set up a research laboratory at the University of Minnesota. His department arranged for him to take over an environmental chamber with the capability to manipulate heat, cold and humidity; other research space was provided as well. The studies we carried out focused on the development and evaluation of an innovative physiologically based liquid cooling/warming garment for space purposes, which Vadim designed. These types of protective garments are worn under the large white space suits astronauts don for space walks. Our research, with the help of university students under our supervision, assessed thermal physiology, subjective comfort and other factors to determine the garment's effectiveness.

Projects with 3M continued, and we tested in our laboratory a newly designed 3M respirator mask. Vadim and I also set up a small business to promote technology transfer from Russia to the United States. However, I continued my efforts to obtain the interest of various US government agencies in funding a Chernobyl research project and, in the process, arranged for Vadim to give presentations on his Chernobyl experiences at different federal agencies. In addition, Alexei Gavrilov from the Institute of Physiology in Belarus was making good progress on the pilot study of radiation fears in two Belarus villages.

I spoke with staff at the National Institute of Environmental Health Sciences about the project we were interested in doing and also about the research possibilities related to collaborating with the staff at the radiation center I had visited in Chernobyl. I was quite amazed to be told that they would have an interest in evaluating a proposal on radon in basements but not major radiation accidents, despite the 1979 Three Mile Island radiation accident in Pennsylvania. It therefore appeared that the most promising route was to submit a proposal through the National Institute of Mental Health (NIMH) and to include in the proposal a section on population health monitoring.

Along with personal reasons for coming to Minnesota, Vadim remained highly committed to maintain his ties with the Center and to obtain funds for Chernobyl research. He felt that he was in a better position to be of help to the Center in providing financial support through the United States than if he had remained in Russia. In addition, the MMPI-2 translation project was still ongoing. Over time, our University of Minnesota Press contact was getting restive about the Russian standardization of this measure, although I reminded them that an entire country had disappeared while this research was in progress. I assured them that the research was moving along, but it would take a bit more time to complete the project. However, it seemed that it would be helpful if I made another trip to Russia to have a closer involvement in the Chernobyl and MMPI projects.

12

MOSCOW AND MINSK TRIP

1994

To finalize details for a Chernobyl grant proposal, the Center staff obtained a visa for my return to Russia. It might have seemed foolhardy for me to travel to Moscow at this time, considering the anger at many levels because Vadim had stayed on in America. However, both of us wanted to see a Chernobyl project reach fruition. We considered that if indeed the Center staff had obtained a visa, there was no danger in my returning, even knowing the disruption that Vadim's departure had caused.

The Center was quite different from what I experienced 1.5 years previously. There now was an operational rather than a research focus to the Center. The new director, Dr. Stefan Grechko, was a surgeon and a colonel in the Russian army. Instead of the huge bust of Lenin at the entrance to the Center during Soviet times, I was bemused that there now was a large picture of Grechko on the wall. Military vehicles were parked in front of the Center and men in military uniforms were active in the building. However, most of the staff that I had worked with on my previous trips were still there, and I was very excited to see both Vasili and Kristina again.

The meeting at the Center was quite tense because they were very upset that Vadim had not returned from Minnesota; however, they still were interested in the possibility of research collaboration, and that was the focus of our conversation. Anatoly, the director from Archangelsk, was in Moscow for some other meetings, and I was so pleased to have a chance to see him again as well.

That evening, Vasili and Kristina took me to a very nice restaurant in the Moscow Arbat district. Now, instead of being chauffeured to different places in a car, we rode in a Center ambulance! Kristina and I joked about our mode of transportation, but the driver was a bit puzzled when he found out what we were talking about. He seemed rather hurt and said that it really was a very nice ambulance.

On this visit, I was housed at the large and quite new Ismailovo Hotel adjacent to Ismailovo Park, one of the largest parks in Moscow. It was a beautiful area; many people were out walking and enjoying the shashlik barbequed by vendors in the park. The hotel lobby was a flurry of activity, full of men from different regions of the former Soviet Union, many wearing track suits. (Apparently track suits were the clothing of choice of the Mafiosi.) There were no food choices for breakfast, so whatever the waiter brought out, that was breakfast. Even though I still did not eat meat, I was hungry, and as I sat at the table and looked at what had been served to me, my thought was "I can't believe I'm eating a sausage and brown-looking cooked cabbage for breakfast," but that was what I ate.

As I was eating, the waiter came over and whispered in my ear, asking me if I wanted to buy a jar of black caviar. This is such a delicacy which I really savored, and I asked him how much it would cost. He said, "10 American dollars," which was an unbelievable bargain, so we surreptitiously made the "deal." It was a win-win situation for both of us, because a jar of the size he sold me would have been tenfold in price somewhere else, and in return, he was thrilled to receive 10 USD in hard currency.

When Vasili came to meet me after breakfast, he was stopped by a security person as he entered the lobby. He was restricted to waiting for me near the front desk—people from Moscow were not allowed to move freely within the hotel. Vasili was very unhappy with the hotel, saying that it was filled with Mafia people. He arranged for me to move to his sister's apartment the following night, which indeed was a more congenial setting. The apartment originally belonged to Vasili's parents. His father had been a well-known professor in Moscow, and the spacious apartment was filled with books. His sister was very friendly and talkative, and we had some nice conversations together.

Vasili and I talked about the progress on MMPI-2. The translation was now complete and he was in the process of collecting standardization data from different groups, including cadets at an air force academy. In addition, the translators at the Center, at my request to Vasili at a previous time, had completed a Russian translation of the Multidimensional Personality Questionnaire (MPQ), developed in my department at the university.

The plan was to travel to Minsk by train to meet with Valentin Gavrilov, the director of the Institute of Physiology in Belarus, to finalize details for the Chernobyl grant proposal. Vasili was my escort, as usual. Vasili's son met us at the train station in Moscow and brought him his treasured video camera. At the other end, Valentin met us upon our arrival in Minsk, and we drove around the city for a short time, then went to his apartment for dinner.

Both Valentin and his wife Elena had different experiences during World War II. Valentin, then a small boy, and his mother were interred in a concentration camp; Elena's father had been an army general who had commanded about twenty-four thousand troops. Elena was very gracious and dignified and an excellent cook. Their teenaged younger son Sasha came home at some point during the evening, and Valentin kept admonishing him to go to his room to study for an important examination that was coming up. (Sasha is now a professor at a prestigious College in London.)

The hotel arranged for me was in the center of the city; Vasili stayed somewhere else. The next morning, Valentin picked me up and we went to the Belarus Institute of Physiology, and Vasili met us there. There was a large portrait of Ivan Pavlov on the wall in the entrance corridor, totally what one would expect at a physiology institute in the former Soviet Union and a definite contrast with a portrait of Lenin. We met with some of the institute scientists, including an older gentleman who held the prestigious title of Academician.

Valentin updated us on the status of the pilot research that Alexei had carried out and the plans for the statistical analyses. The pilot study clearly demonstrated the long-term concerns of the villagers about the personal and family health effects of the Chernobyl disaster. This result was seen even among the adult and adolescent groups informed by the government that they were living in an uncontaminated village. There was considerable distrust of the information provided by the government and a realistic uncertainty about the ultimate health outcomes from the disaster. These concerns had a negative impact on their daily physical and mental health. We felt that the findings from our study provided a scientific rationale for conducting a large-scale study of the mental health of the Chernobyl population.

Together with the Gavrilovs and Vasili, we worked out as many of the details as we could think of to include in the proposal that I would submit to the NIMH, including the budget for the additional very basic equipment they would need in Belarus, such as computers, supplies and a fax machine. The plan was for the Moscow Center and the Minsk groups to work together on the data collection. I explained again the procedures for submitting a grant proposal, the peer-review process and the probability of approval for funding. I emphasized that of course we were all hopeful of obtaining funds, but there was no guarantee.

Minsk is a beautiful city with stately old buildings, and Valentin took us to a museum and other attractions of the city. That evening, Valentin and Elena took me to a ballet performance at the National Opera and Ballet Theatre of Belarus. It was a lovely, elegant performance, so reflective of the love of the ballet in the countries of the former Soviet Union.

The following morning, we met up with Vasili and drove to the Gavrilov's dacha, not far from the city. Their dacha was really impressive, on two levels and with wood paneling everywhere. Valentin told me he loved to fish, and he took me out on his rowboat for a ride around the lake the dacha was situated on. He barbequed skewers of shashlik, and the tradition of camaraderie and toasts to friendship continued.

When we returned to Moscow, one of the people I wanted to visit was the mother of my Minnesota Russian helper and friend, Misha Arkharov. Misha's wife Nina and daughter Anna had by this time joined him in Minnesota, but he had not seen his mother Ella in several years. Vasili and I took several buses to reach the apartment she shared with her husband. Ella was an outstanding scientist who had been part of the Soviet team that developed the equivalent to the Salk vaccine to prevent polio. She was now retired and told me that for the entire time that she had worked professionally, she saved money to supplement the pension she would receive upon retirement. However, with the still extremely poor economic situation in Russia, the entire amount that she had saved, in her words, would only buy a few grams of kielbasa. This was quite a sobering and sad revelation. Nonetheless, we had a delicious dinner that included Siberian pelmeni and sour cream, which I love.

The following and my last evening in Moscow, expeditioner Dmitry invited Vasili and me for dinner and arranged for a driver to pick us up and take us to his apartment, which was a bit far from the center of the city. We had a very pleasant, joyful evening. His wife Tatiana is a fantastic cook and prepared a lavish meal. Dmitry went down twice to talk to the driver who was waiting for us, and asked him to come up and eat dinner with us. But the driver, I assume, was rather in awe of Dmitry and stayed in the car. Dmitry's apartment was on two levels, and finally he was able to get his rather shy younger son Matvey to come up and say hello. It was amusing to see the way Dmitry affectionately pinched his son's cheek as he talked to him.

Dmitry was full of plans for the Adventure Club, talking about potential places for expeditions for the disabled. He also was organizing a summer camp for teenagers that would be held in the Arctic, to promote peace among young people from different Arctic countries. Dmitry had many contacts in the United States and Canada related to his expedition and other projects, and I knew that we would see each other again in Minnesota at a future time.

(The expeditions with disabled people that the Adventure Club later carried out included a successful climb to the summit of Mt. Kilimanjaro and another to the summit of a mountain in Central Asia. The Adventure Club continues to run international summer camps for teenagers to promote peace, now with his two sons taking on major responsibilities.)

Moscow was changed in many ways at the time of this visit. This was the period of "wild capitalism," and people, irrespective of their profession, wanted to do "beezniss." One of the psychologists at the Center who also had been involved in the MMPI project was now traveling back and forth to Central Asia and China buying goods to sell in Moscow. Vasili referred to him as having become a "criminal."

It was with a bit of a feeling of relief when I boarded the plane for Minneapolis. I had to do an overnight stop in Amsterdam to connect with my flight the next morning. While I had confidence that I would not have any problems in Moscow because of Vadim's decision to remain in Minnesota, one could never be entirely sure. I phoned Vadim as soon as I got to my hotel in Amsterdam, and then I went out for a stroll and to find a restaurant for dinner.

13
EPILOGUE

Vadim and I worked together at the University of Minnesota for many years. Sadly, we were never able to get a proposal funded for Chernobyl research, although we continued these efforts for several years. Our joint research was centered on the development of the physiologically designed shortened liquid cooling/warming garment for astronauts. We received a patent on this design, shared with the university. We named the garment the MACS-Delphi (Minnesota Advanced Cooling Suit-Delphi). The MACS part was the idea of our NASA project director Robert Treviño; the Delphi part was Vadim's poetic contribution.

Vadim and I published numerous papers in scientific journals on our space research and on topics of disaster management, and we presented these findings at national and international scientific conferences. Vadim also served on several national and international committees tasked with developing guidelines for population protection from nuclear, biological and chemical agents. He headed the World Association of Disaster and Emergency Medicine's (WADEM) Nuclear, Biological, Chemical (NBC) task force, and I organized and headed the WADEM Psychosocial task force.

In 1996, we organized a disaster conference at the University of Minnesota titled "When Everyone Leaves – Mid and Long-Term Effects of Disasters." This conference was extremely well received and was perhaps the first to focus on the extended physical and mental health effects of disasters. Four people from the Center, including current director Stefan Grechko, attended and did presentations.

Over the years, Russian friends came to visit, including Vasili, who stayed for three weeks at our house and attended an MMPI conference in Minneapolis. Dmitry came multiple times, as did Vladislav Brabec and his wife Bojena from the Czech Republic. Valentin visited from Minsk and his son Alexei also visited several times. I still stay in touch with Dmitry, Alexei and the Brabecs.

Through NASA and university funding, Vadim and I maintained an active research program focused on the development of protective clothing for space purposes. Vadim directed the Laboratory for Health and Human Performance in Extreme Environments at the university, and we supervised both exercise physiology and psychology undergraduate and graduate students, and a postdoctoral fellow. We also worked with a pediatric surgeon on some physiological design applications for stabilizing core temperature in infants undergoing surgery.

However, it also was a bittersweet experience. Before leaving Russia, Vadim had the personal approval of President Yeltsin to stand as a candidate for Minister of Health. It was not that easy in the United States, and sometimes one makes decisions based on the heart rather than the head.

Our friend Anatoly Tkachaev died from an unusual type of tumor at the end of the 1990s. With his work and exposure to radioactive soil and other environmental contamination after Chernobyl, I still wonder whether that exposure eventually produced the lethal tumor he developed. Vadim's health deteriorated badly during the last seven years of his life, and he died in November 2018 from a progressive neuromuscular disorder that had aspects of a Parkinson's disease syndrome. Similar to Anatoly, while it was never possible to make a direct connection between the radiation he was exposed to at Chernobyl and other highly contaminated sites and his illness, the somewhat atypical pattern of his symptoms left unanswered questions.

I have continued to conduct international research on expedition teams and have maintained an active involvement with NASA's Human Research Program, serving on advisory committees in the team and behavioral performance area. I currently am part of a US-Russian collaborative research project involving a mixed-gender group of three American and three Russian participants who will live and work in the simulated Mars habitat chambers in Moscow for an eight-month period. The Russian participants will be administered the translated Russian MPQ personality measure that Vasili was key in developing.

Figure 2. Presentation of the findings of my psychological research on the Bering Bridge expedition team members at Moscow Center in Fall 1989.

Source: Photo courtesy of Gloria Leon.

Figure 3. Trip to the Institute of Ecological Problems of the North in Archangelsk in 1990, hosted by Director Professor Anatoly Tkachev.

Source: Photo courtesy of Gloria Leon.

Figure 4. Standing with my driver and guide in front of Chernobyl Building No. 4, enclosed by a sarcophagus following the disaster; I am wearing protective clothing in this 1992 photo six years post-explosion.

Source: Photo courtesy of Gloria Leon.

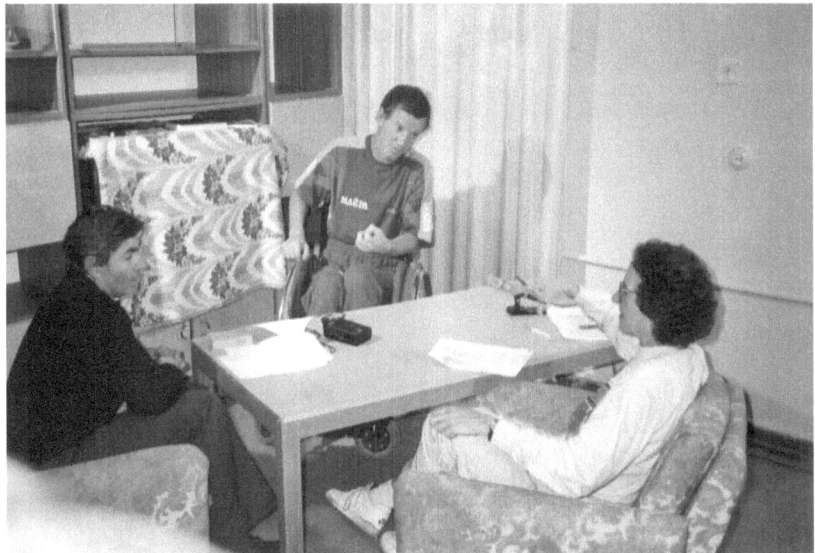

Figure 5. Conducting an interview at a children's center in Ryazan, Russia, with a disabled participant in the 1992 15,000 km wheelchair expedition organized by eminent Russian expeditioner Dmitry Shparo.

Source: Photo courtesy of Gloria Leon.

EXPEDITION ADVENTURES

14

STEGER INTERNATIONAL POLAR EXPEDITION

1986

My first opportunity to study an expedition team came about in a serendipitous way, as research sometimes happens. I heard from a colleague that members of a soon-departing expedition team were coming to the University of Minnesota for physiological tests—body composition, oxygen capacity and strength measures. I quickly said, "Wait, don't let them get away until I have a chance to talk with them." I saw a very unexpected and exciting opportunity to carry out a comprehensive psychological study of the team, starting at this pre-expedition point, then continuing the research during and post-expedition. The more details I heard, the more interesting a psychological study became.

I had always been a "tomboy," active in sports and outdoor activities, and here was a mixed-gender international team of adventurers with the goal of being the first documented expedition to successfully reach the North Pole without outside support. Their plan was to travel by ski and dogsled, carry all of their food and gear and use a sextant for navigation.

I rushed over to the research laboratory where the testing was taking place and introduced myself to Will Steger, the expedition leader, co-leader Paul Schurke and the others; I described the research I was interested in doing, and the rationale. I explained that my focus was on a better understanding of the personality characteristics of people who volunteer for physically challenging and potentially dangerous undertakings, and also to systematically study team relationships in extreme environments. The group was interested and in fact a bit flattered that I saw a scientific justification for their expedition, in addition to their own historic/adventure goals.

The entire team (seven men, one woman) completed the pre-expedition personality testing and were diligent in filling out a rating form each evening on the ice. The rating form included questions about mood, interpersonal relationships and work performance. The team successfully reached the North Pole in 56 days; the final sprint required a tremendous amount of physical exertion, despite the very small amount of food left in the last days of the expedition.

When the team returned to Minnesota, I did semi-structured interviews with each of them at my university office. At each interview, I received their dog-eared paper questionnaire forms that often had coffee stains and other marks on them (I didn't think about what the other "additions" might be). One fact that I learned from this first expedition study was to use pencils to do the rating forms; the ink in ballpoint pens freezes in the extreme cold.

The personality findings and the daily questionnaire each member completed during the trek were very interesting and reflected a mature, psychologically well-adjusted group. The individual personality profiles showed that they were not high risk takers looking for death-defying experiences; they were individuals with a moderate level of risk-taking characteristics (adventure-seeking), low stress reactivity and good coping skills in dealing with different kinds of stressful situations. The group had high scores on a measure of achievement motivation, suggesting that the attraction of the expedition was in the challenge and reaching a desired goal, not in the risk aspects.

The post-expedition interviews provided more context and additions to the questionnaire data. Team members talked about leader versus follower roles, as well as other types of roles within the group. One member had been a leader of a previous expedition; however, he said that his role on this expedition was to follow the leader's direction and not challenge authority.

The only woman on the team indicated that one of her roles during the trek evolved to providing social support to the others. This process likely was facilitated by the fact that she was in charge of administering first aid as needed; however, the conversation in this and other situations sometimes took a more personal direction in terms of "home" or other matters. On the other hand, she felt that while she ended up in this social-emotional role, only the co-leader was interested in hearing about personal issues she was experiencing during the trek. Her experience was not unique; women in extreme environments often report having not only the burden of their own concerns but also the added emotional burden empathizing with the problems of others in the group.

15

EXPEDITION NETWORK

Following this first expedition study, I then was "in the loop" with expeditioners, many of whom are from Minnesota where dogsledding is popular. Just three years later, co-leader Paul contacted me and described the plans for a Soviet-American Bering Bridge expedition. He asked whether I wanted to study this group. I was very pleased that he had asked me, and I immediately agreed. Of course, I didn't realize it at the time, but the outcome of my involvement in this expedition changed both my personal and professional life.

I have continued doing research on expedition teams from the time of the first Steger–Schurke North Pole expedition. This research program has included studies of single-gender (including three all-women Antarctic expeditions), mixed-gender, civilian and military national and international teams, all doing treks in either the Arctic or Antarctic. For many years, I was the only scientist in the United States conducting systematic studies of expedition teams.

As the American space program progressed over time, consideration of psychological factors during space flights took on more prominence. Dr. Al Holland, a psychologist at the NASA Johnson Space Center, read my expedition studies published in scientific journals and invited me to participate on a committee he was organizing. The committee was tasked with recommending a battery of psychological measures to evaluate both NASA and Russian crews for the upcoming Shuttle/Mir missions.

From that point on, I considered my expedition research in the context of an analog for a space mission. I wanted to identify personality traits related to optimal functioning in a highly challenging situation and also individual differences in coping methods, team interpersonal and work performance, and decision-making processes. Over the years, my collaboration with the NASA Human Research Program (HRP) has included membership on advisory committees and serving on and chairing peer-review panels that evaluate research proposals. I also served on several

National Academy of Sciences advisory committees assessing NASA's research progress in the human performance area. And it all started with dogsleds, skis and a few people!

There needs to be a certain joy in doing research; like any other activity, parts of the work become routine and sometimes rather boring. Writing grant proposals to obtain funds to conduct research and receiving the required approval that the research meets ethical standards can take an extremely long time. Inputting data onto spreadsheets or running numerous statistical analyses also can get rather "old." But the interest in the potential scientific findings overrides the tedious aspects. Also, as an expedition research "junkie," there is always the adventure if you can actually travel to the vicinity of the expedition, meet the expeditioners and do the debriefing interviews on-site. And after the science part is finished, then it is possible to enjoy chats with the team and maybe have a drink together.

I have had the incredibly good fortune of being able to meet up with a number of expedition teams in distant and remote places, just as they were completing an expedition or a prolonged stay in a polar region. These trips have taken me to many places in Russia, above the Arctic Circle in Alaska, Nunavut territory in Canada, England and three trips to Greenland.

16

SOVIET-AMERICAN BERING BRIDGE EXPEDITION

May 1989

The 12-person Soviet-American Bering Bridge expedition consisted of six Soviet (five men, one woman) and six American (four men, two women) Caucasian and indigenous team members. The vision driving the expedition was to promote Soviet-American harmony by opening up the Bering Strait area so indigenous people on each side of the international border could communicate and trade with each other. The border had been closed since the time of the Cold War, separating families on either side of the border. The expedition began in March 1989 from the Chukotka region of the Soviet Far East and ended in Alaska, having covered over 1,600 km. The team made planned stops at villages along the way; they gave formal talks about their hopes that the expedition would result in greater international awareness of the plight of the people in the Bering area and that changes would occur.

This expedition study provided me with my first opportunity to travel to the site of the expedition, in this case the ski finish in Nome, Alaska, and then north to Kotzebue, above the Arctic Circle. The expedition plan had been to ski all the way to Kotzebue, but this was not possible because of the melting ice. In order to reach the original end point of the expedition, after the stay in Nome, the team planned to fly to Kotzebue for ceremonies commemorating the official end of the expedition.

I flew to Nome via Anchorage, having timed my flight to arrive in Nome a day before the team was set to arrive. Nome is located on the coast of the Bering Sea and accessible primarily by airplane; it became a major gold-mining area following the period of the Klondike Gold Rush. Currently, Nome is best known as the finish line of the Iditarod dogsled race.

This small town was incredibly depressing. When I arrived, I saw intoxicated people, mostly men, everywhere. At the hotel I stayed at, people were collapsed at tables and sprawled in the window wells of the restaurant/bar area. However, with the imminent arrival of the expedition team, there was a flurry of activity and excitement as journalists, community leaders and townspeople gathered to greet the team.

The atmosphere in Nome became quite frantic with all of the celebration activities and the number of visitors there. The team members were very happy and relieved to have successfully reached the end of the skiing part of the expedition; they fully enjoyed the music, dancing and adoration of the children and adults. Of course, in this atmosphere it was rather difficult to organize the final psychological testing and interviews. With co-leaders Dmitry and Paul's help, I was able to do some of the interviews in Nome, and I completed the rest in Kotzebue, flying with the team on their chartered flight. The research scientists from the United States Army Research Institute of Environmental Medicine (USARIEM), also studying the expedition team, brought along a great deal of equipment for their physiological research. They were under a tight time schedule, but they were able to complete their physiological studies in Nome.

The team spent four days in Nome, so I had quite a bit of free time to see the area. I walked down to the shore and just stared out at the Bering Sea, still quite full of ice. It was very cloudy that day, and the sea did not look inviting. I also hooked up with two photographers from National Geographic, and we roamed the area in their rental pickup truck. There definitely were a lot of dog kennels to visit, as many of the mushers live in this area.

Several times I rode along with Lonnie, one of the expeditioners from Minnesota, and accompanied him as he made the rounds each day to feed his dogs. He had a sack of frozen salmon that he chopped into pieces with an ax and threw to each dog, separately chained to a stake in an area away from town. Hmmm … gourmet dog food. I really had fun riding around in these pickup trucks with these new companions, observing a totally different way of life from that of my own experiences.

Finally, it was time to fly to Kotzebue, a community 53 km north of the Arctic Circle on the Bering Sea. The Inupiat town serves as a trading center for the region. It was now May, but in this far north area, there still was snow on the ground, although in various stages of melt. It was quite windy and overcast the entire time I was there. Many villagers drove ATVs with family members perched on the back and children on the driver's lap.

I was able to complete the post-expedition interviews on all of the English-speaking team members; I did the interviews late at night, following the village events. Because of Kotzebue's extreme northern location, there was light even at midnight. None of us felt tired, so the interviews proceeded smoothly. Maxim Abramov, the Soviet researcher from Magadan in the Soviet Far East, completed his studies as well.

There was a large cooperative in Kotzebue, some shops and, to my surprise, a small Chinese restaurant. Maxim and I had dinner at the restaurant one evening and walked around the village. He was intrigued with the variety and amount of fresh oranges and other fruit available in the cooperative, unlike the situation in Magadan. Maxim had a video camera with him and filmed the fruit and produce in the store.

The entire expedition team, entourage and local Alaska officials were in a wait mode. Seventy-six Soviet dignitaries were scheduled to arrive on two Aeroflot planes for the closing ceremonies, but as always, the weather held the upper hand. After a two-day delay, the delegation from the Soviet Union arrived; they had US Department of State permission to remain in the United States but for only 6 hours! However, that was enough time to hold the planned ceremonies, and the Soviet group departed later in the day.

While in Anchorage on my way back home, I decided to do a day trip to Valdez on Prince William Sound. The devastating Exxon Valdez oil spill had occurred just a few weeks earlier. When I arrived in Valdez, all I could see were masses of people, pickup trucks and tents set up right on the roads. It must have been what the boom towns in Alaska looked like during gold rush days. People had come from all over the country to land lucrative jobs working on the cleanup.

I spotted a large building with a restricted sign on it that was a rescue center for the waterfowl and sea mammals that had been contaminated by the oil. I walked over to the building, simply stated to the person at the door that I was a professor from the University of Minnesota, and they let me in and gave me a tour of the facility. Many young and obviously dedicated people were carefully trying to clean oil off of the feathers of the birds and ducks that were caged there. It was a very sobering experience; I empathized with these teams of workers trying to save these beautiful delicate creatures. However, given the extent of the spill, they would be able to save only a relatively few. But the contrast—Prince William Sound is spectacularly beautiful, and it was so good to gaze at the scenery when I walked some distance away from the town. Toward late afternoon, it was time to get back to Anchorage for my flight home the next day.

There was a wealth of data that I collected over the course of the expedition, and the in-person interviews always provided new information. The major findings, not surprisingly, pointed to two different ways team members carried out their tasks; a more cooperative group approach among the Soviet team and a more independent one among the Americans. There also was a cultural difference regarding the attitude toward the three women on the expedition. The American women said that they expected to be treated as equals and felt put down when a Soviet man offered to carry part of their load. However, the Soviet men felt that they needed to protect the women and were being good teammates by offering to help.

Disagreements between the Soviet and American co-leaders on daily plans or other issues created a negative emotional climate; some members indicated that they were torn between siding with their national leader on a particular issue or the other leader with whom they agreed. There were other factors as well that influenced team dynamics; the overall mood of the team was strongly related to the progress they made that day on the ice. While stopping in villages along the way was a major goal of the expedition, it had a negative impact on team effectiveness; while indigenous team members were with the villagers, the others were left to pack up camp. However, the camaraderie in the tents in the evening, including guitar music and songs, was a strong factor in promoting team harmony and alleviating some of the stress that might have been experienced that day.

17

ALL-WOMEN EXPEDITION (AWE), SOUTH POLE

November 1992

I was definitely in the expeditioner network. Ann Bancroft, a Minnesota team member on the 1986 Steger International Polar Expedition, contacted me and asked whether I would be interested in studying a four-woman expedition team she was going to lead on a traverse of the Antarctic continent. I jumped at the chance and invited Pauline Maki Kahn, a graduate student in the clinical psychology program, to work with me on this project. We developed the specifics of the research protocol and put together the questionnaire materials the team would carry with them in their gear, carefully compiling the forms in a binder that would be as lightweight and compact as possible. I also contacted the team members, sent them the pre-expedition personality and other questionnaires, and asked them to return the completed forms before they departed on the expedition.

The team participants that I had a chance to meet prior to the expedition were friendly, cooperative and very enthusiastic about their involvement. (I really envied them. I wish I could have been in their shape to do this exciting adventure.) They were quite interested in the research, and it was a great experience to meet with them and review the instructions for completing the daily expedition measures on the ice.

The team traveled on skis, hauling sleds that weighed up to 90 kg; they reached the South Pole in 67 days, having covered 1,126 km. However, it was becoming questionable whether the full team would be able to successfully accomplish a full traverse of the continent; two of the members were having severe physical problems—one, chronic bronchitis and a sprained ankle; the other, chronic fatigue.

As the team got closer to the South Pole and the physical problems of the two participants became more intense, the group had a discussion every evening—whether the members having difficulty should be flown out at the South Pole and the rest continue on, or whether the entire team, in solidarity, should stop at the South Pole, still having attained a significant feat. There were differences of opinion, but Ann, the leader, made the extremely difficult final decision that the team would stay together and finish the expedition at the South Pole. Although quite disappointed that the expedition had to end in this way, the entire team accepted this decision and remained a cohesive group. A plane was dispatched to pick them up, and they flew from the South Pole to Punta Arenas Chile and then on to the United States.

The team arrived on a flight to Minneapolis and were transported directly to the Ramsey County Medical Center in St. Paul, where Pauline and I were waiting to conduct the debriefing interviews. It was a testament to the team's research commitment that the first member who walked through the door spotted me and said, "Oh no, I forgot to complete the questionnaire this morning." What an example of commitment!

Pauline and I analyzed the study data, showing that the AWE team was a well-functioning group; they worked together and communicated with each other in an effective manner. Interpersonal stressors were the most frequent type of stress mentioned, related to concerns about their teammates; a frequently reported coping strategy was to focus on the meaning and the goal of the expedition. The maturity of individual team members was reflected in their agreeing, without divisiveness, to give up their own ambition to traverse the Antarctic continent in order to allow all team members to share in the same achievement. The fact that the team did not splinter into factions showed their concern for each other and acceptance of a modified meaning of the expedition, that is, reaching the South Pole together.

Overall, the research results showed that this all-women's team was similar in work performance to all-men or mixed-gender teams, although more sensitive to problems a teammate might be dealing with. The prominence of interpersonal concerns evident among members of the AWE group has been documented among women in a number of expedition studies.

18

SVERDRUP CENTENNIAL EXPEDITION, CANADA

June 2000

The one-year Sverdrup Centennial expedition was organized by Graeme Magor, a Canadian physician, athlete and expedition history buff. His dream was to retrace the sea route from Norway to the High Arctic of Canada that famed Norwegian explorer Otto Sverdrup had carried out a century earlier. Graeme's plan included a land expedition on Axel Heiberg Island to search for a cairn that Otto Sverdrup had deposited at that time to claim sovereignty. The experience of living in the most isolated and remote region in Canada inhabited by families was another objective of the expedition.

Graeme formed an international group consisting of three married couples (Canadian; New Zealand/Canadian; Norwegian). Graeme and his wife Lynda's 2.5–year-old daughter Keziah were included as well. Most of the group sailed across the Atlantic Ocean on a small 16.5 m boat; Lynda and Keziah joined the boat in Greenland for the rest of the voyage. The Norwegian couple shipped their two large dogs to an Arctic village in Canada and picked the dogs up along the way.

The group arrived at their destination, Hourglass Bay on Ellesmere Island, in early August, harboring at a latitude of $76°\ 23'$ N and a longitude of $87°\ 50'$ W; shortly thereafter, the ice completely froze and the boat was icelocked until the following August. From the end of October until mid-February, the group lived in a progression of darkness/light, including a six-week period of total darkness.

As soon as the group arrived at Hourglass Bay, they began constructing a small hut about 500 m from the boat as a safety backup. With the availability of the hut, another benefit was that couples were able to rotate between living on the boat and the hut. The dogs stayed on the ice close to the boat and served as watchdogs for bears; they also hauled the sledge on the later land journey three of the group embarked on. However, because of numerous polar bears in the area, the group had to stay close to the boat or hut and always needed to carry a firearm for protection.

I heard about the Sverdrup expedition from my friend Liv Dahl, who was a heritage specialist and a journalist with the Sons of Norway organization in Minneapolis. I quickly suggested that I contact Graeme to find out whether he would be interested in participating in a psychological study of their expedition and, if so, to find out from the rest of the group whether they were interested as well. This also would be a great opportunity for Liv; she would have direct experience with the expedition for the articles she would be writing for the Sons of Norway newsletter. Liv thought this was a very good idea as well.

Graeme was quite enthusiastic about the possibility of a scientific study of their expedition and having Liv gather the information she needed for her article; the others also agreed. Graeme told me that he would arrange for us to fly up to the boat on the resupply plane from Resolute, Canada, in early April and stay on the boat and do the interviews in person. There were sleeping quarters available on the boat for each of us, and after I completed the research tasks, someone from Grise Fiord would pick us up from the boat and drive us on their snow machine to Grise Fiord. There were flights from the village to Iqaluit, and from there we could connect to Ottawa. What a fantastic, exciting opportunity. This was total research accommodation! I mailed copies of the pre-expedition questionnaires to all participants and asked them to mail back the completed forms before the start of the expedition, and that is how the research began.

Liv and I flew to Ottawa, stayed overnight and then flew on Canadian North Airlines to Resolute, 5 hours northwest from Ottawa. I gazed at the attire of those getting on the plane. While the temperature in Ottawa was fairly mild, most of those boarding carried heavy parkas that they stowed in the luggage racks.

The plane made a stop in Iqaluit, a small, primarily Inuit city that is the capital of Nunavut territory. It was a strange feeling to get out of the plane, look around and realize how far north we were. We saw mostly indigenous people in the terminal building. There was a hospital close by and a number of administrative buildings near the terminal. The area around Iqaluit was of great strategic importance during World War II and the Cold War; the United States built an American airbase in Iqaluit, and the large airstrip built at that time now serves as the Iqaluit airport.

On to Resolute. The plane descended into an intense snow storm and wind; the runway was quite icy and the pilot pumped the brakes several times to avoid skidding off the side of the runway. I noticed a man in an aisle seat a few rows ahead of us literally holding the seat arm with a white knuckled fist, but Liv and I, perhaps in our ignorance, simply looked out the window.

Someone from the small hotel we were staying at (one of only two hotels in Resolute) met us at the airport and helped us with our duffel bags. Resolute is situated on the Northwest Passage and came into existence in 1947, also for strategic purposes during the Cold War. The United States and Canada built a weather station and a large airstrip; a Royal Canadian Air Force base is located there as well. Because of the excellent communication system and weather station, Resolute also serves as the operations base for North Pole expeditions. This small village is divided into two parts, the military presence near the airport and the Inuit homes, school, clinic and town hall on the other side of the village.

Because of the severe weather conditions, Liv and I stayed at the hotel for three nights before we were able to fly to the boat on Ellesmere Island. A number of times, the weather cleared in Resolute but the snow and related visibility was still poor at Hourglass Bay, and vice versa. Over the course of our stay, we got to know all of the people at the hotel, some expeditioners and others in the village. The very hearty meals at the hotel were served cafeteria style, and we sat with others at large tables. Everyone was very friendly, wondering what on earth we were doing up there. We chatted with the hotel manager many times. She was very dedicated to her job in Resolute despite the fact that her husband had died of a heart attack within the past year, which she said he would have survived if there had been a hospital in Resolute.

There were several men at the hotel and in the village in various stages of frostbite and other injuries, who had to be evacuated from North Pole treks because of their injuries. Liv and I were a sympathetic ear, and they were interested in hearing about my previous expedition research. We also met an Inuit woman who was the mayor of a village south of Resolute; she had been to Iqaluit on indigenous tribe business and now was waiting for a different flight to get back to her home. She was eager to show us the black leather gloves she had bought in Iqaluit.

We walked around the village and had an interesting time talking with the teacher and seeing the school and community sports hall; the children were all smiles and looked very healthy and robust. Then, on to the town hall and the small clinic. The nurse told us that she "babied" the injured, exhausted and disappointed expeditioners who had to be evacuated from the ice; she washed their hair and provided tender loving care for their frostbite and other injuries.

Liv and I were really getting into this village walkabout. Another day, we decided to visit the air force complex. Why not? There we were introduced to a member of the Royal Canadian Mounted Police, and, no, he was not wearing a bright red jacket and a large white hat. He had on a dark blue uniform, and his mount was his snow machine. A huge padded orange jacket was part of his outerwear.

With my background of research on protective clothing for space purposes, I was quite interested in how he could keep warm on his snow machine as he made his rounds of the territory in brutal cold weather. He took off his jacket and showed me the lining. I was amazed; the lining consisted of at least 6 cm of thermal insulation, and, of course, in extreme cold he would be wearing many layers of thermal clothing underneath. I lifted up the jacket and indeed, it was really heavy! There also was a jail in the building, and to end our inspection, our new Mountie friend showed us the two cells.

Finally, the weather cleared in both locations and someone on the hotel staff was notified. He told us to quickly get ready, and he would take us to the airport. Also, the mayor had lost one of her prized new gloves; the staff person gave us the glove and said that someone would pick it up from the boat. He also gave us a few cartons of soft drinks to bring to the Sverdrup group.

Liv and I were very excited about this next adventure—the flight, arriving at the boat and meeting everyone. We flew out on a Kenn Borek Air charter flight. Twin Otters are called the workhorse of the Arctic for very good reason; the planes are able to get off the ground from a short snow-packed runway and ascend almost like a helicopter. The planes also can land in unbelievably tight spaces.

The Kenn Borek Air company has a stellar reputation, having carried out rescue flights not only in the Arctic but also in Haiti, the Antarctic in total darkness in winter and other places. These bush pilots are just fantastic. They understand weather conditions, and by looking at shadows on the ice, know exactly where there are bumpy areas and thin ice. You definitely wouldn't want a commercial pilot trying some of the landings these pilots do routinely with ease.

Now our journey was taking us still farther north to the boat icelocked in Hourglass Bay on Ellesmere Island. The plane was filled with food, fuel and other goods for the Sverdrup team and would return to Resolute with empty fuel cans and other discards. The copilot alerted us when we were close to our destination, and as I looked out the window from high up, I saw what seemed like two black sticks sticking up from the ice. As the plane descended, I saw that these sticks actually were the masts of the sailboat. Then we had a clear view of the boat, a bit sunk into the ice.

We were greeted upon landing by an entourage of people, empty fuel cans and other containers; there were lots of greetings between the pilot, copilot and the Sverdrup group. Very quickly, Keri escorted Liv and me to the boat while the rest of the group helped offload the supplies and then load on the discarded items. Canadian Keri and her New Zealand husband Greg owned the boat and made their living taking groups on sailing adventures to remote places.

My first close impression of the boat was how small this 16.5 m boat was to sail across the ocean, and now at Hourglass Bay, to have this many people living on it. I noted a trench chopped into the ice around the boat; its purpose was to protect the hull so it would not be crushed by the ice. Once inside the boat, Graeme gave us a safety talk and then we were shown our snug berths. Liv and I were quite amused that Keri had placed chocolates on each of our pillows! The chocolates were donated by a Canadian company, and there was a plentiful supply onboard.

Later, all of us gathered in the cozy saloon for some snacks and drinks and to get to know each other a little better. Graeme and Lynda's young daughter Keziah was jumping all around and proudly showing us her stuffed animals. Lynda was a teacher; during her stay on the boat, she developed an expedition educational website program to which all of the others contributed. Guldborg and Lars were from Norway, and the youngest couple in the group. Lars had a PhD in geophysics and was evaluating an acoustical method to determine snow properties of the adjacent region; Guldborg was working on a doctorate in biology and was collecting plant and soil samples for her dissertation.

Following the main meal, Liv brought out a wellwrapped package that contained three cake layers, individually wrapped. She expertly put this special Norwegian cake called *kransekake* together, added frosting and then placed little flags on top of the now ascended cake. The flags represented each of the countries of the people on the expedition. It was a very pleasant and festive way to begin our stay on the boat. Before going to our berths, Graeme again reminded Liv and me about the dangers of polar bears and that we should never leave the boat without one of them being with us.

We worked out a schedule for the interviews that would begin the next morning. The schedule was fairly structured because the walls of the boat were quite thin, and in order to have privacy, the others needed to do activities outside of the boat. However, since the Magor family was living in the hut at the time for their 7.5-week rotation period, I did their interviews in the hut, without disrupting the others.

I conducted all of the interviews on the boat sitting on the bed in my berth with the interviewee sitting across from me, also on the bed. This was the most private place on the boat. When I rather amusedly commented to Lars at the end of our interview that this was a first for me, interviewing someone while sitting on a bed, he looked a bit startled, not realizing that this comment was meant as a joke. All of the interviews proceeded quite smoothly. People spoke softly to maintain privacy, and I felt they were quite open in expressing both positive and sometimes negative interpersonal experiences. Keri was quite talkative and I needed to keep her on track a bit to deal with the relevant interview material. It took two days to do all six interviews; because of ongoing chores, it wasn't possible for people to be away from the boat for long periods of time. Over those first days, however, everyone found their own private time to complete the additional psychological measures I brought with me.

I was rather envious of Liv because she was able to do a few short excursions from the boat with her countrypersons Guldborg and Lars. But on the third day of our stay, now that all of the interviews were completed, I had an opportunity to see more of the area. Liv and I walked with Keri and Graeme on the twice-weekly trek to the communications tent located on land about 1.5 km from the boat. It was an incredibly awesome and beautiful experience to see this unending expanse of white, ice crystals glistening in the sun and surrounded by very small rolling hillocks. Liv and I checked out the inside of the communications tent, and Graeme explained the setup that enabled the team to send email messages from this location. As Liv and I started to walk down a small hill near the communications tent, Keri cautioned us not to walk anywhere without her and her firearm. She said there could be a bear resting in a hollow at the bottom of the hill that we would not be able to see from the top. Helpful advice for sure!!

We all relaxed after the interviews were completed, not having to worry about schedules, and I so enjoyed the excellent camaraderie and simple but very healthy and tasty meals. Keziah was rather a distraction at times, demanding attention, but for the most part (except for Lars), it seemed she added to the positive spirit of the group. There was a definite routine to life on the boat, with lots of effort each day concentrated on the protection of the boat. Each person had set chores, although cooking and cleanup duties were rotated; however, Keri and Greg's primary duties were centered on maintaining their boat.

One afternoon, we heard from afar the noise of an engine, and soon a snow machine appeared alongside the boat. It was the husband of the mayor we had met in Resolute! It was a bit of a story, showing how people living in these very remote regions communicate with and help each other. At the hotel in Resolute, his wife was in the shower when the call came to quickly get to the airport for her flight to her village, but she did not hear the phone ring and missed her flight. Her husband had to pick her up via snow machine to bring her home, which was about a 5-hour one-way trip. Then the lost glove. Someone told her that we had brought the glove to the boat.

Therefore, her beleaguered not-very-happy husband on another day drove yet another long distance to the boat to pick up the glove. Graeme told him there was room for him to sleep overnight in the boat; however, he demurred. He made a bed for himself in the komatik (Inuit sled with wooden runners) he pulled behind his snow machine and spent the night there. Graeme told me later that he felt the man did not feel comfortable sleeping below water level. The komatik is a very useful mode of transportation in this Arctic environment. It is large enough to carry fuel cans and other gear for long trips over the ice, and provides a place to sleep.

Too soon, it was time for Liv and me to get ready for a long snow machine ride to Grise Fiord and from there fly to Iqaluit and then on to Ottawa. Graeme had made arrangements for an outfitter from Grise Fiord to drive out to the boat with expedition weight clothing for each of us for the very cold 5-hour ride to the village. I was sure that my so-called expedition weight Columbia parka would be warm enough, but the others agreed that I would need something warmer for the ride.

A teenaged boy duly arrived on a snow machine, bringing along two sets of clothing—polar bear fur pants, seal skin gloves and mukluks, and a huge, heavy parka that someone had to hold over my head to pull down. There was great deal of hilarity all around as Liv and I were outfitted in all of this gear; everyone took pictures, there were big hugs with everyone and then we were on our way. I sat on the snow machine seat behind the driver, and Liv sat behind us in the komatik.

Over this extended "voyage," we noisily raced over the shining endless expanse of ice, my arms around the driver's waist, occasionally having to grab harder when we went over some rough ice and the vehicle seemed a bit airborne. And there was Liv, bouncing behind us in the komatik, where she said she preferred to remain. We stopped a few times along the way to drink some warm tea our driver brought along, but Liv and I were a bit wary of drinking too much and then having to make a pit stop, which boggled the mind with all of the clothes we had on. When we pulled in to the shore at Grise Fiord, we urgently asked where we were staying, and then Liv and I made a frantic dash for the washroom. Liv was by far much faster than me on this race!

Grise Fiord on Ellesmere Island was an intriguing place to spend some time, and we had a chance to mingle a bit with the local Inuit villagers. Grise Fiord is the northernmost and coldest inhabited village in North America and has a very sad history. The settlement was created in 1953 by relocating eight Inuit families from a northern area of Quebec in order for Canada to maintain sovereignty of this area during the Cold War. The families were made promises that there would be shelter and other amenities when they arrived at Grise Fiord; there also was a promise, but later withdrawn, that they could return after a year if they did not want to stay there. Basically, however, they were dropped off at this site, there was nothing there and they were left to fend for themselves for survival. It is a testament to their traditional subsistence hunting and fishing skills that they survived.

The small lodge in Grise Fiord where we stayed for two nights was very comfortable, although the woman at the desk kept admonishing us to take off our boots, even before we were totally inside the door (she likely was thinking about our mad dash to the washroom). After we got settled in, we had a great time walking around the village and getting a feel for the life there. The brightly painted village houses all had a doghouse out front and usually a large piece of meat drying on a rack outside.

We walked past the cooperative, town hall and a church, and went inside this small church. On the wall facing the door, a flyer was posted encouraging people to attend alcohol and drug group meetings. Another flyer announced a meeting on depression and suicide, which the community seemed vulnerable to considering the long winter darkness and isolation, during which our driver told us there was absolutely nothing to do in the village.

A very large iceberg about 200 m from the shore faced the village. A festival had taken place near the iceberg over the previous days, and there were remnants of the festival yet to be removed from the ice. The next day, Liv and I decided to take a walk around the iceberg and have a different experience from being on the ice seated on a vehicle. It seemed safe because of the evidence of people activity that was still scattered on the ice, such as chairs and tables. When we returned and mentioned this to a woman at the cooperative we were talking to, she was surprised that we had gone out there alone, because of the ever-present danger of polar bears. So we were quite fortunate in our ignorance.

The cooperative was the center of the village, stocked with food, clothing and whatever hardware or equipment one would need to live in this environment. We went over to the cooperative both days; it was really interesting just to hang out there. Many of the women who waited at the cashier line had babies on their back in a papoose inside their parka hood. But the transition of a culture was evident. On our second day there, the woman standing in line in front of me was greeted by the cashier, who asked her how she was. She responded that she had been staring at a computer the entire day and was feeling really spaced out. The cashier then asked her if she had any plans for the weekend, and she enthusiastically said, "Yes. I'm going on a polar bear hunt!"

In the evening, we walked over to a community room where a group of teenagers was playing loud music and dancing. Even though the temperature was well below freezing, all were wearing short sleeve T-shirts. Our snow machine driver, whose father worked for the provincial government, was there as well and gave us a hearty greeting. He was telling us about a vacation that he, his parents and two siblings were going on, and my thought was "oh, they're going to ride on their snow machines and visit relatives or friends in another village." But no, what he said was, "We're going to Disney World!" I clearly was rather snobbish in my surmise of the location of their holiday.

Reluctantly, because Grise Fiord was such an interesting and remote place, the next morning we gathered our belongings for the short ride to the airport for a Twin Otter flight to Iqaluit and then on a larger plane for the flight to Ottawa. The very short runway area in Grise Fiord is bordered by mountains, both on one side and at the end of the runway. These barriers require the pilot to make a hairpin turn to land, and only highly experienced bush pilots are able to do this.

There were several villagers, who were flying to Iqaluit for medical appointments, waiting with us for the plane to arrive. Upon boarding, I saw that there were only several rows of seats toward the back of the plane; the passengers in front were dogs in several cages on the floor. There was a curtain at the back of the plane behind which was a bucket for biological urges. We had about an hour's wait at the airport in Iqaluit, both of us savoring these last images of a civilization that was so different from our usual life. Eventually, our plane arrived, and we flew on to Ottawa and the end of this incredible experience.

One of my aims for doing this study was to apply the findings from a group of people living and working together in an isolated and confined environment to crews living and working together during space flights and on planetary surfaces. Back at my office, I worked with Mera Atlis, a graduate student in the clinical psychology doctoral program, to analyze the questionnaire data I had collected. We also tried to identify specific themes from the comments made during the interviews.

The study results clearly showed that the social support a couple provides to each other is highly important for the harmony of the entire group. Several reported that this support by their partner was a significant and effective way of coping with the stresses experienced. Following occasions when there were disagreements with others in the group, a person could confidentially confide their feelings and concerns only to their partner. This also lessened a need to confront the person(s) one had difficulty with. Effective coping methods such as the use of humor and planful problem-solving were mentioned as well.

The mood and behavioral data showed that the isolation and the period of darkness was not a stressful time, contrary to some of the scientific studies of personnel in the Antarctic. For this group, the darkness period, particularly at the beginning, was a quiet, tranquil time, with both positive and negative moods reduced. Perhaps this was similar to what the Danes call "hygge." In terms of carryover knowledge for space purposes, having at least one crew member with whom one can confide in seems extremely helpful in reducing stress and maintaining harmony and positive performance over an extended duration mission.

19

TWO-WOMAN ANTARCTIC TRAVERSE

November 2000

Seven years later, Ann, the leader of the AWE expedition, contacted me again; she and a Norwegian partner, Liv Arnesen, were planning a two-woman ski traverse of Antarctica. Their goal was a sea-to-sea trek, traversing from Queen Maud Land, in the north, south to McMurdo Base, located at the end of the Ross ice shelf. She asked whether I would like to do another study in which she was a participant. I was very pleased that she had contacted me and told her so, and I began working out the research details. Mera, who had worked with me on the Sverdrup expedition, was interested in collaborating with me on this project as well, and also Gro Sandal, a professor, friend and colleague from the University of Bergen.

We followed my usual research protocol consisting of pre-expedition personality and attitude questionnaires, a weekly rating form completed on the ice and a debriefing interview upon return. We focused in part on team dynamics in a dyad with different cultural backgrounds. Also, I was intrigued by the "sensed presence" phenomenon reported by some Antarctic expeditioners during the Heroic Age of Antarctic Exploration, the period between the late nineteenth century until the end of World War I. I included items on the rating form to assess whether these experiences had occurred while Ann and Liv A. were on the ice.

Mera and I had the opportunity to meet with both teammates prior to the start of the expedition. To prepare for the trek, they trained separately as well as together, and we met with Liv A. in Minneapolis. The two women were very complementary to each other in several ways, although different in behavioral style. Both were former teachers and had considerable expedition experience; they also were close in age. Ann was of medium height, average body mass and very outgoing. Liv A. was quite tall, more slender and reserved in expression, consistent with a Scandinavian cultural stereotype of emotionality.

The teammates worked together on the trek in a highly productive way, in part reflecting their teaching backgrounds. With the help of base camp staff, they carried out a website educational program that included daily communications to schoolchildren all over the world. They hauled sleds loaded with their gear and skied 2,861 km in 97 days. A unique aspect of the expedition was their use of windsails when conditions were favorable; however, there were many days when they could not ski because of severe blizzards. These delays put them under considerable time constraints, in terms of their planned return from Antarctica.

Ann and Liv A. had arranged to meet up at a ship that would be close to McMurdo Base on a specific date and then travel on this vessel to Australia. But in order to meet this timeline, they were forced to end their trek at the edge of the Antarctic land mass; a plane picked them up for the remainder of the journey to McMurdo Base, located on the ice shelf. Therefore, while successful in reaching the edge of the Antarctic land mass, they were extremely disappointed that they had not accomplished their sea-to-sea expedition goal. But what an accomplishment they did make!

I met with Ann and Liv A. in New York two days after they returned from Australia. I booked a room at the same hotel they were staying at and set up a table in my room to do the individual debriefing interviews. The differences in their personal styles were quite evident; Ann knocked on my door with a big smile on her face and gave me a hug; Liv A. looked a bit tentative. However, after each formal interview was completed, it was very enjoyable to spend a bit of time one-on-one, just chatting. It seemed that by the time they got to New York, their disappointment in not reaching their stated goal was lessened to a certain extent by the significant accomplishments they had made.

My interview with Ann revealed that she actually did have a sensed presence experience on the ice. She told me that as she was slogging along in a very white and barren environment and feeling quite tired, she suddenly felt her deceased grandmother's presence over her shoulder. She said that her grandmother had been a rather stern but loving person, and Ann really felt that her grandmother was there with her. She heard her grandmother's voice repeatedly telling her to keep on going, not to give up. While there have been many theories about the mechanism that produces this hallucinatory experience, it certainly had a positive effect in motivating Ann to keep moving and endure the strenuous terrain. Perhaps the key factors in producing the experience are low sensory stimulation from the environment, combined with extreme physical fatigue; however, there still is no consistent agreement among professionals about the cause of this phenomenon.

In my experience doing expedition studies, the results from a specific expedition always provide insights that can be applied to other settings. This study showed that it was possible for two teammates who were co-equal in age and prior expedition experience to live and work together in a cooperative and efficient way, without having to designate one of the members as the leader with decision-making authority. Scores on a measure of verbal aggression were low for both team members; also, the importance of adequate and clear communication in maintaining effective team performance was evident in their comments and behavior. Both had similar approaches to problem-solving, stating that discussing task concerns with each other was a frequently used method of coping with stress.

While the environment at times was extremely challenging, awe and enjoyment of the environment were mentioned by both teammates as highly positive features of the expedition and sources of psychological strength. Mood ratings during the trek showed individual differences in the range of positive and negative mood states, likely related to both temperament and culture.

Over the years, Ann and Liv A. continued to organize and participate in different types of expeditions. Their overriding goal was to include international groups of girls and women on treks across the polar ice, to provide these female participants with a personally empowering experience.

20

GREENLAND STUDIES

Daneborg Station, June 2012

I first heard about the Danish military Sirius Patrol and their activities in Greenland from an email message I received from Torben Eriksen, a Danish man who had served in the Sirius Patrol during the 1950s Cold War period. He contacted me after reading an article about my research that was published in *Popular Mechanics Magazine* (an interesting venue for a psychologist, but the article centered on applications of my expedition research for space purposes). Torben described the history and current activities of the Sirius Patrol, a special forces military group that monitors the northeastern part of Greenland via dogsled and skis. He thought the isolation, extreme environment and activities of the Patrol could serve as an analog for a lunar or planetary mission. I was very intrigued by the possibility of studying this group, and I followed up with an email asking for more information.

The Sirius Patrol is a highly prestigious special unit of the Danish military, based in Greenland and formed during World War II to monitor German weather stations and ship activity. At the present time, the Patrol's primary mission is to maintain Danish sovereignty by patrolling the northeastern uninhabited national park area of Greenland, covering approximately 18,000 km of coastline. The Patrol members are selected following a stringent down-selection process; applicants pass through a series of physical and psychological tests, followed by observation during a winter training period.

The location of the Patrol in the isolation of Greenland, and the fact that 12 people divided into two-man teams live and work together in this extreme cold environment for prolonged periods of time, suggested its possibilities as an analog for space missions. Each team usually consists of one "old guy" who is starting his second year of deployment and one "new guy" who is just beginning his stint.

The teams go out on patrol for extended periods, hauling most of their gear with them on dogsleds. They set up tents each night, except for times when they stay in huts along the way where they can shelter, sleep and replenish their food supply from the cache stored there. Each team covers between 700 and 1,500 km on the 7-week Fall journey and between 1,800 and 3,500 km on the 24-week Spring journey. The teams return to their Daneborg base before Christmas and then go out again for the Spring journey at the end of January. Torben commented that what expeditioners were doing as an adventure the Sirius Patrol does as a daily work assignment. I certainly could see interesting possibilities in studying these teams.

Torben has proven to be an amazing resource and help. He knows the history of the region thoroughly, having worked in Greenland for many years. When I expressed my interest in studying the Sirius Patrol, he immediately focused on identifying the appropriate contacts in the Danish Arctic Command; after he had made the initial contact, he sent me the names and email addresses to follow through. It did not take long for Torben to get a response. I followed up with the commander in Greenland and sent him the proposed study protocol.

The research tasks involved completing psychological questionnaires before the start of the Fall journey and again at the end of the Spring journey. While on patrol, they would be asked to fill out a biweekly rating form that takes about 10 minutes to complete. I proposed that if feasible, I would come to their Daneborg station in Greenland and do the post-expedition debriefing interviews when they returned from their Spring journey.

The communications with the Danish Arctic Command went along very smoothly; I received a number of impressive emails signed by "Michael," with the Danish royal crest on it. I was given official permission to do the study, but with one stipulation, that I would not become the third member of a two-man team! I assured Michael this was "no problem." I then began communicating directly with Daneborg station.

There is an open email system at the station, and before too long I received a message from a patrol member named Anders Kjærgaard; he had read my message and responded, stating that he wished to work with me on the Sirius project. He wrote that he had an undergraduate degree in psychology and would be attending graduate school when his term of service in Greenland was completed. I was delighted with this development; to have on-site help with logistics and other matters from someone with a psychology degree and experience as a patrol member, and then to continue working together, was a very good happening.

I flew to Copenhagen to meet with Anders when he returned from Greenland, to work directly with him on the study protocol. I didn't know what he looked like as I waited for him at the set time in the hotel lobby. Soon, this extremely tall man came bursting through the door, blond hair flying and sporting a full beard, surely a giant Viking. There certainly was no question who this person was! We immediately hit it off, and soon we were talking like old friends. After our conversation in the hotel, Anders suggested that we take a walk around the area. We stopped at Amalienborg, the Royal Palace, just in time to see the changing of the guard. Anders told me that earlier in his military service, he had served as one of the palace guards, marching in the formal parade at the changing of the guard.

Based on the aims of the research, we discussed the relevant personal and team factors to include as items in a biweekly rating form that would be a variation of the rating forms I used with previous expeditions. We also worked out the logistics of getting the materials to Daneborg, having the Sirius Patrol chief oversee the research and maintaining confidentiality among team members.

The plan was for Anders to take care of photocopying the questionnaires and send them on to Daneborg in 12 individual folders, one for each of the men, on one of the early Fall flights. Andreas, the Patrol chief, would then distribute the materials to the team members. Anders proposed that the confidentiality issue could be solved easily when the teams returned from the Fall journey. They could place their data in a safe at the station that only the Patrol chief had access to, and collect their materials when they returned in June from the Spring journey. Anders took primary responsibility for the translation of the various measures.

It appears we set a precedent—as I involved my aunt with professional skills to work on the Russian questionnaire translations, Anders's aunt, who was an English teacher, worked on the Danish translations. In addition, Torben helped out a great deal. We followed the standard procedure of a back translation of every item from Danish to English to ensure that the items translated into Danish retained their original meaning.

I remained in Copenhagen for a few days to do some sightseeing. The Hotel Opera where I stayed was located just off of Nyhavn, the picturesque canal and harbor area. As usual, I greatly enjoyed people watching, and it was fun just to sit and relax. I also took a long walk to see the mermaid statue. How could one be in Copenhagen and miss that? I had dinner at the Café Petersborg; a guidebook indicated that in years gone by the restaurant had been a favorite of Russian sailors. I ordered the three-herring appetizer, with great thick bread and a beer. Life doesn't get better than that!

The next day, I took a train a short distance from Copenhagen to see the Karen Blixen (Isak Dinesen) home and museum at Rungsted, north of Copenhagen. I was able to look across the waterway to Helsingborg, Sweden, and glimpse the Kronborg (Hamlet) Castle. I was really charmed by the countryside, and the houses and farms I saw along the way. As a Blixen fan, it was a special experience to visit the manor house that she returned to from Africa, browse in her study and walk through the grounds. I tried to visualize her life there and, of course, how different the setting was from Africa. I now was ready to return home and continue with the Daneborg plans via email with Anders.

The project moved along smoothly thanks to Anders's direct contact with patrol chief Andreas. The Year 1 new guys completed the pre-expedition questionnaires before they left for Daneborg; the Year 2 old guys, already in Greenland, completed the questionnaires before they left on the Fall journey. With the project underway, Anders and I communicated as needed with Kent Rønshøj, who was the head of the Stations and Patrol Service Greenland and in charge of overall selection. Kent was stationed at the Danish Air Force headquarters outside of Aalborg, Denmark; the initial plan was that I would fly from Aalborg to Daneborg on a military flight after the Spring journey.

There were a number of flights to Daneborg in June to resupply the station. Maintenance personnel and scientists also were accommodated on these flights; however, the flight schedules ended up being quite flexible because of weather conditions and other factors. I was quite elated when Kent approved travel to Daneborg for me and for Birgit Fink, who was assisting me on the project. We had to complete some forms for permission for this travel to a military facility, and everything was taken care of in a very smooth manner. Birgit is a great friend and companion; she carried out an undergraduate research project at our space suit laboratory at the University of Minnesota and quickly transitioned from being a student to a true friend and colleague.

To my surprise, however, it turned out that we would not be leaving from Aalborg on a huge C-130 Hercules cargo plane but on a Twin Otter, my favorite plane, from Akureyri in northern Iceland. Wow! We were both amazed and delighted that we now would be traveling not only to Greenland but to Iceland as well. We worked out an itinerary to stay in Reykjavik for a few days and then fly up to Akureyri for our flight to Daneborg.

I arranged for a rental car at Keflavik Airport in Iceland. Birgit was very keen to do the driving, so I had the good fortune of just sitting back and being the passenger. We walked all over Reykjavik and took long drives in the countryside. We were quite taken with the small Icelandic horses with their shaggy manes and the beautiful flowers in the fields. Birgit had a friend in Reykjavik whom she hadn't seen in many years. We met for dinner and had a very nice time together. Her friend worked for a bank, but ever since the devastating 2008 financial crisis in Iceland, she had to commute each week to Oslo for her job.

Birgit and I did the Golden Triangle tour, a drive through a geothermic area with geysers and the huge, spectacular Gullfoss waterfall. We also drove to the Blue Lagoon near the airport and swam in the thermal heated waters (we certainly were trying to make the most out of our time in Reykjavik!). The area between Reykjavik and the airport made me think of what the surface of a planet might look like—barren ground with a few plants sprouting up, covered with black lava in an undulating pattern. From the viewpoint of the road, the lava extends across the land as far as the eye can see; in the other direction, the lava covers the ground all the way down to the sea. This is truly the country of fire and ice.

Our next adventure was the short flight from the domestic airport in Reykjavik to Akureyri in northern Iceland. The city is located on a fiord and is surrounded by gorgeous glaciers. The temperature was quite a bit cooler and windy compared to Reykjavik, but we were well prepared with our thermal wear for Greenland. We just walked and smiled as we strolled through the center of town: colorful wooden buildings, two gigantic wooden trolls, male and female, standing in the middle of the walkway mall and creative displays in the shops. There also was a statue to lost sailors. We had dinner at a restaurant on the top floor of a building overlooking the water, where a cruise ship was docked. We had memorable meals of fresh fish and fancy desserts and were totally happy to be in this city, even for a short time.

We arranged for a ride the next morning to the airport and just waited for someone to appear in a uniform, we presumed, to tell us what to do (go with the flow, my motto). Our instructions were quite vague, but a Danish military officer eventually appeared, along with some young women who were graduate students at Lund University in Sweden. The students were traveling to Greenland to spend the summer working on their own research projects. The officer kindly bought sandwiches at a vending machine for everyone to take with on the plane (oh yes, this is not a commercial flight with meal service).

A Twin Otter duly rolled onto the tarmac, and we were on our way. It was a clear day, and as we neared the coast of Greenland, beautiful mountains and glaciers came into view that became even more spectacular the closer we got. We landed for refueling at a place called Constable Point, an outpost with large oil tanks and an official office, where we had to show our passports. The area was quite desolate, and I marveled when one of the men told me that he just loved the place; there was a nice apartment building and he had lived there for 12 years. After the refueling and a bit of chitchat, we were on our way again.

I was wearing headphones, and when the plane descended, I didn't hear what anyone said, but I thought we were dropping off the students from Lund first at another station in Greenland. As I walked down the stairs of the plane, there was someone waiting to say hello, but I didn't realize we were actually in Daneborg. His accent was a bit different than Anders's, but then, rather embarrassed, I realized it was Andreas, the Patrol chief who was saying hello. Quite soon, several vehicles arrived to offload supplies, and two of the guys came over and carried our duffel bags on the walk to the main part of the station.

Birgit and I were shown to rooms in the Aktiviteten building, which also included a large room with an array of fitness equipment. We were given bed linens and towels, and told the time for dinner. Our rooms were, in our view, absolutely perfect; there were typical Danish (of course) cabinets, a narrow bed and impressive scenery to gaze at from the window. We never had trouble sleeping despite the 24-hour daylight. Throughout our stay, we kept marveling at how beautiful Daneborg was, both the outside setting and the building where we were housed.

Daneborg is located on a peninsula at 74.3° latitude. There was a large boat on land near the airstrip; in the summer, the boat ferries supplies to the station and is used for recreation. There are a number of wooden buildings spread out over the area; Sirihus is the main building and includes the kitchen and dining area, lounge and a communications and airport operations center. The barrack buildings were further back from the shore, and all had views of this truly lovely mountain/glacier environment. There was an entire area filled with dog kennels. We smiled at the many dogs simply sitting on top of their kennel and enjoying the scene; there was lots of activity and noise when the guys went out to feed their dog teams.

Andreas had posted a schedule for the interviews that were to begin the same evening we arrived. Birgit and I, laptops in hand, got organized in a small nearby building called Axelborg. I set up my laptop on a desk that faced a large chair where the interviewee would sit; Birgit sat at a table behind me to type the interview responses and any additional comments. I brought along a bag full of earbuds and pens to give to each of the guys after their interview. I also took their picture at that time, so we could keep straight as to who was who. There always were cans of soft drinks stocked in the Axelborg building, and sometimes someone left coffee as well. (We kidded them—just like room service!)

Andreas scheduled himself for the first interview. He seemed a bit nervous at first as he faced these two ladies from America, but then he relaxed and appeared comfortable with the interview questions. Birgit and I continued working nonstop over the next two days to complete the interviews with the 11 guys who participated in the study. Considering the stereotype of the Silent Dane, these guys were super talkative and we were really pleased with that.

It turned out that each interview was running about 1.5 hours. I expect the word got around that we were not asking for a lot of very personal information, and the guys on the whole seemed to enjoy the experience of having two women to talk with. We had one last interview remaining to do on the third morning. We did a soft drink celebration with Peter, the last guy, after we were finished.

For the rest of that day, we were free to wander around and get a bit of a feel of the activities on the station. Andreas admonished us repeatedly not to wander out of sight of the main building because there were polar bears in the area. It was interesting just to observe what was going on. The guys were casually dressed and everyone was on a first name basis. Each of them had their own ATV to drive to the different parts of the station where they were working. At one point, two of the guys wanted to move a picnic table up to the Sirihus deck that was a floor above ground level. It turned into a big operation, centering the table just right onto a forklift, then raising the table above and over the railing and on to the deck. Birgit and I carefully observed this entire procedure, wondering whether it might have been easier to simply carry the table up the stairs to the deck.

The Sirihus building, along with everything else at the station, was spotlessly clean and organized. Inside the Sirihus entrance, there was a coat rack on the wall with each person's name above a hook. When we went into the dining area the first evening, Birgit and I just took seats at the table, but later we realized that everyone had their own specific seat. The guys (and us, as we learned the routine of the station) stood until Andreas gave the order to sit down; at the end of the meal, following whatever instructions he needed to convey, all got up from the table the same time he did. There was a small bar adjacent to the dining area, but for the most part, none of the guys took drinks. The refrigerator in our barracks was stocked with beer, but again, drinking was quite minimal and each person paid for whatever they drank.

The men took turns clearing and washing the dishes, and Birgit and I helped out as well. We noted how well stocked the pantry was with food, which made me understand why Andreas refused the already "worn" shrimp salad sandwich I had offered him when I got off the plane, thinking that these guys would be hungry for something different to eat. It was a lot of fun to be part of the camaraderie in the kitchen as we worked together. Toward the end of our stay, Birgit and I helped out dusting the lounge and washing the floors, as the group prepared for the upcoming Year 2 traditional parents and friends' summer visit. Birgit got very enthusiastic with the dusting, and for sure everything she touched was totally clean when she had finished.

Troels, the youngest guy, gave us a sightseeing tour of the station. I was very impressed with the amount of winter clothing gear, skis, camping and other equipment there was in stock. We also visited the sewing hut and saw for ourselves how self-sufficient these guys were. Each of them made their own large backpack and other personal gear for their journey; they also built their own sleds, a quite detailed and expert undertaking. One building was a clinic that served for dogs as well as people. Troels showed us an adjacent room where a sick dog was lying in a cage. He said that a veterinarian from Iceland would fly up to Daneborg as needed to care for the dogs; the dogs, of course, were a crucial part of the Sirius Patrol undertaking.

The last buildings we visited, a bit further from the main complex, were Hotel Karina, a hut that had been the dwelling of a fur trapper, and another hut that was a small museum. There was a small grave nearby, dated 1942. On the way back to the main area, we noticed blood on the snow near one of the buildings. Eydfinn, a patrol member from the Faroe Islands, had gone ice fishing and caught and butchered a seal, which provided food for the dogs.

Our last full day at Daneborg fell on the date of the annual Sirius barbeque, a major patrol festivity. There was a lot of activity as the guys set up a barbeque outside one of the buildings near the runway and brought out a side of a pig to roast. Andreas told Birgit and me that this was a very special guy event and that we were not to roam around but to stay in our quarters, lest we happen on a polar bear. This was a bit strange, but we were guests at Daneborg, and of course we followed the rules. The next morning, we understood why we were admonished, as we saw the guys in various skimpy costumes and, I presume, some hangovers, awaiting the arrival of their parents and friends for their summer visit.

The visitors had flown from Aalborg to Mestersvig Station, south of Daneborg, in a C-130 Hercules cargo plane. The gravel runway at

Daneborg was not as large as the one at Mestersvig, so the group needed to change to a smaller Twin Otter to fly to Daneborg. They were delayed for quite a while because of bad weather, but eventually they arrived; it took two trips to get everyone from Mestersvig to Daneborg.

There was no room for Birgit and me with the arrival of the families. Plans had been made for the two of us to fly back to Mestersvig on the Twin Otter, bringing along two retired sled dogs that would become pets for the two-person team that manned Mestersvig. However, before the Hercules arrived, Andreas told us the adage, "Never strip the bed until you see the plane's wheels touch the ground." He said that the schedule for our return to Denmark kept changing because of the weather, but in some way, we would get to Aalborg where we had arranged to meet with Anders. Certainly, with all of my expedition travel, I know that the weather is the rule, and the timing of eventually getting to Denmark would happen when it happens.

Birgit and I took our last looks at Daneborg before getting on the plane. The location and station itself are so impressive in every way, and both of us wanted to imprint the sights we had of the gorgeous scenery and the people we met there. We were in Greenland, just a vast expanse of white when flying over it at 10,000 m on a commercial airline, but so lovely closer to Earth. Our pilot and copilot were very friendly, and they helped get the canine passengers onboard. Birgit and I were rather concerned that the dogs would get into a fight with each other on the plane, but all was calm. In fact, the dog that I was holding on a leash spent almost the entire flight looking out the window, as was I!

Mestersvig Station is located at latitude $72°\ 14'$. The flight south took us over the most breathtaking scenery yet, mountains, glaciers, frozen lakes, all glistening in the sun (Torben was right when he told me many months previously that the view would be absolutely spectacular.) But the scene as we landed at Mestersvig was very different compared to Daneborg. There is a large airstrip area and a long gravel runway to accommodate the C-130 Hercules and other large cargo planes. Our first impression was of the numerous oil storage tanks and cans scattered along the shoreline, and several large trucks parked in the area. Some of the buildings were made of metal siding, and the wooden buildings showed their wear.

There was a large building where the two station personnel lived; the aircraft and other communication systems were inside. We saw men in hazmat suits driving to the station complex from an area where, we were told, there were abandoned mines; the men were working to clear the ground contamination in the area.

Our sleeping quarters were in a wooden building that contained five separate rooms. Upon entering the building, we noted furniture, some broken, stacked along the walls and in some of the rooms. The décor included a large ax on the wall enclosed in a glass container. Each room had bunk beds, pillows and comforters. We were given sheets, pillow cases and a towel for our use. I noticed that the comforter on the bed I was making had a large bloodstain on one side, so I switched with a comforter on another bed.

I was already set up in the room when one of the pilots came in and thought this was supposed to be his room. Birgit and I had been told to take any room we wanted, so he rather reluctantly chose another room in the building. The toilets and sinks were located in a large steel shipping container near our barracks; the showers were in another steel shipping container, with a bit of an unstable sloping floor. Birgit and I just smiled and decided we were not going to take any showers while we were there.

Dinner was served in the *kantine* building that also had a foosball table and some lounge chairs. Birgit and I were elbow to elbow at dinner with about ten Icelandic men, who were clearing the decontaminated areas. The food was good. There was not much conversation at the table while people ate their food.

Afterward, one of the men offered to drive Birgit and me out to the cleanup area to show us around. We hopped into the pickup and saw that the windshield was completely covered over with mud and grit; there was no visibility whatsoever. Our "tour guy" wasn't totally familiar with this vehicle, and he kept looking for the switch to turn on the windshield wipers. After many tries, he still couldn't find where it was. So reliable Birgit jumped out of her seat, went around to the driver's side and immediately found the switch. He was a bit embarrassed, but he made up for it by telling us many details about the history of the mining in that area, and we walked close to one of the mine shafts. From what we saw of this site, it seemed that it would take a very long time to return this area to a less contaminated state. Back at the *kantine*, there were many people in the lounge area, including our pilots, and it was a nice relaxed way to end the day.

The following day, we simply waited to hear the plans for getting to Aalborg. We stayed in the *kantine*, spread out the questionnaire materials and worked on the data coding. Because of weather and other factors, the plans kept changing, several times over the course of the day. The final plan was that the next day we would fly to Keflavik Airport in Iceland on the same Twin Otter that brought us to Mestersvig, stay overnight in

Reykjavik and then fly commercially to Aalborg via Copenhagen. All the flight bookings and the hotel in Reykjavik were arranged for us through an office of the Danish military. Yet again, we were so impressed and grateful for the care with which we were treated.

The next morning, our pilot friends, Birgit and I were getting prepared to leave. As we walked over to the plane, we saw the pilot carrying rows of seats onto the plane and locking them in place. We joined in to help, and it was quite a different experience to actually be changing the interior of the plane we would be flying on, from one set up for lots of storage, to now simply serving as a passenger plane. We were the only passengers on the plane, so definitely we were riding in style. We arrived at Keflavik, and Birgit and I took a shuttle to our hotel. We were quite happy to have this unexpected chance to have more time in Reykavik; we just wandered around, enjoying the people and the beautiful views.

Next was a travel day, with a long wait at the airport in Copenhagen for the flight to Aalborg, but eventually we got there and settled in at a hotel adjacent to the Aalborg Congress and Culture Center. Anders had been kept informed about our itinerary. He now was a graduate student at Aalborg University and immersed in his studies in the organizational psychology program. That evening, Anders rode over to the hotel on his bicycle to say hello, and we related some of our impressions from the interviews. We all had a very pleasant time sitting with beers on comfortable chairs in the hotel lobby, just chatting away.

Later that evening, July 3, Birgit and I took a walk around the center of the city. We were quite bemused to see small American and Danish flags hanging from wires strung across the narrow cobblestone streets. We found out that there is a long history of friendship and close relationships between Denmark and the United States. Since 1912 and except for the World War II years, the Danes have held a several-day outdoor festival near Aalborg to celebrate the Fourth of July as a sort of homecoming for Danish Americans, expatriates and the Danes. The following evening, July 4, we saw a large crowd in tuxedos and gowns entering the concert hall near our hotel for a celebration. The Danish friendship for Americans also is evident in the main square of Aalborg, named John F. Kennedys Plads.

The next day, we talked more formally with Anders about the statistical analyses and the focus of the manuscript write-up. I suggested that I return to Denmark when the initial analyses were completed; I thought it would be valuable for Anders and me to present the study findings directly to the military psychology section group involved with the Sirius Patrol. After our meeting with Anders, Birgit and I had the rest of the day free. We had planned for a few extra days as a backup for our trip, knowing that the weather and other factors would determine the time of our exact return to Aalborg.

Aalborg is a charming city on a fiord, located in the Jutland region, the northernmost part of Denmark. I got to know it well over the course of my continuing Greenland projects. The central city is full of historic colorful houses, narrow cobblestone streets and a castle located close to the waterfront. There is a large mall complex adjacent to the central square with a cinema, shops and a supermarket.

I always like walking through local grocery shops when I travel to foreign countries; seeing the types of food local people eat is one way of getting a better idea of the culture and lifestyle. I was rather amused and took some pictures of two large refrigerated cases containing only jars of different types and preparations of herring. My kind of place! (The breakfast buffet at the hotel also featured a large array of herring.) That evening, Birgit set up her laptop in the hotel lobby and we continued with our work. We left for the airport early the next morning, and since then, Birgit and I have a standing joke. Whenever one of us says "Mestersvig," we both break out laughing, but it is amusement for a fun and different experience, not disrespect.

The exceptional cooperation of all of the people I dealt with in the Danish military was really amazing and greatly appreciated. Kent at the air force headquarters in Aalborg, Michael in Greenland, the Sirius Patrol guys and the people at Mestersvig all couldn't have been nicer or more accommodating. Anders already was a good friend, totally conscientious and knowledgeable; having been a member of the Sirius Patrol, he had insights concerning the research that were invaluable. Anders and Birgit also had an instant friendship and affinity; Birgit is from Germany and Anders's mother also is German.

The interview findings, as always, were very informative. A two-person team on patrol for an extended period must live and work together in an effective way; this is crucial not only for the mission but also for their personal safety. A major theme, with applications for planetary exploration, was the significance of adequate communication. Team members indicated that it was important to be able to know when to express an opinion or make some other comment, and when not to. They used the expression "swallowing a lot of camels," meaning that sometimes one just had to let some issue go by and not create a confrontation.

Several mentioned the need to clarify what their goals were for being a member of the Sirius Patrol, whether to prove oneself, fame, and so forth, as this would have an impact on their attitude and performance. They felt that understanding their personal motivations would make it easier to deal with the interpersonal or work problems that inevitably occur during the patrol journey or back at the station.

Another theme centered on the interactions between the old guy and the new guy. Initially, there is a leader/follower relationship; however, as the new person gains more experience and confidence, there may be friction unless there is an adjustment to a more collaborative decision-making relationship. This process has implications for long-duration space missions, where, similarly, over time, crew members become more familiar with each other's work and may expect decisions to be made in a more egalitarian manner.

A topic of great significance had to do with influences from home that had a major effect on their psychological health and performance while in Greenland. Because of the long 26-month deployment in Greenland, officially, those selected to the Sirius Patrol do not have a girlfriend; however, five of the 12 patrol members revealed during the interviews that they had a girlfriend who broke up with them while they were in Greenland. This caused major distress for many, and one member had significant difficulty focusing on his work responsibilities because of this distress. This finding has considerable application for the psychological support of astronauts on long-duration missions. It is important for astronauts to have a comfortable and supportive level of communication with the people at home; however, there is a risk when these communications have a negative impact on work performance and safety during the space mission.

Denmark, December 2012

Anders arranged for me to give a presentation on our initial study results to the military psychology group involved with the Sirius Patrol, and we met in Copenhagen. Anders was doing well with his studies and making good progress on his master's thesis. He came to my hotel a few hours after my arrival, we greeted each other as old friends and with no time wasted, we made some room at one of the tables in the hotel common area to talk about the data already analyzed. We worked for several hours and then had dinner at the hotel buffet that was almost adjacent to where we were working. Anders came over the next morning and we spent a good part of the day working together.

That evening, Anders and I had a reunion with Andreas, the Daneborg Patrol chief, now also a university graduate student and working on a master's degree in geography. He arrived at the hotel via bicycle. It was really nice to see him again, and we shared some of the fun experiences Birgit and I had at Daneborg. It was my treat for dinner, and I asked the two of them what kind of food they wanted to eat, actually hoping for some traditional Danish food. Both mentioned an American steak house close by, so that is where we went. I presumed they had enough fish in their daily diet!

Bente Sæmark-Thomsen, the woman who was in charge of the Sirius Patrol selection section, picked Anders and me up the next morning and drove us to Jonstrup, home of the Danish Air Force Officer's School. The plan was for me to do the presentation, and then Anders and I would answer questions and deal with other comments. The talk went well despite the fact that because of jet lag, I only had a total of about three hours of sleep. As always, though, I got a bit carried away during my talk. I started waving my hands around for emphasis and messed up the slide advancements because I inadvertently kept pressing down on the power point remote clicker. (Always a hazard when I give a talk, and Anders came to the rescue.)

The presentation and comment period lasted about three hours, but you do what you have to do, jet lag or not. The adrenaline was flowing strong enough to get me through the formal part of the meeting. After my presentation, Bente presented me with a beautiful Danish glass carafe and glass set, which sits proudly on my dining room table; then we all walked over to another building for lunch. Some of the psychologists were interested in the specific psychological measures I used in my research and the advantages of these measures. We also talked a great deal about the effects on team effectiveness resulting from problems in communication between team members. Among the group, there was some frustration about what if anything could be done to alleviate the potential negative influence of events happening in the home environment.

Following our lunch and more conversation with this extremely welcoming group, one of the Danish soldiers drove Anders and me to an airport for our flight to Aalborg. Anders had arranged for me to do a presentation at Aalborg University the next day on my expedition research program. I was introduced to an audience of students from psychology and other programs, and I was pleased with the positive response to my talk.

One of the men in the audience asked me a lot of questions during my presentation and came up afterward to talk some more. It turned out that Jesper Corneliussen, who was a good friend of Anders, also had been a member of the Sirius Patrol, in addition to having served in the Danish special forces Jaeger Corps. It was interesting to meet him and I certainly remembered him because of his questions and comments. We didn't know it at the time, but it turned out that Jesper would be a new colleague on my future Greenland expedition research.

Anders had a friend and fellow student who had a specialization in statistics. He lived with his wife and toddler daughter in Aarhus, and Anders suggested we drive there and meet with him. We got an early start the next morning; Anders was driving an older car that belonged to his father that Anders used when camping. I was pleased with the opportunity to see more of the Danish countryside on this drive of about 120 km.

We had a good visit with his friend and family, and received some helpful tips on the statistical analyses. Although this was December and rather chilly, the parents wrapped up their daughter in a snowsuit and lots of blankets and laid her in her baby carriage outside for a nap and fresh air. I definitely was impressed with this culture related to fresh air, even in relatively cold weather. No wonder the Danes are so healthy!

Anders, ever the friend, wanted me to see some of the sights of Aarhus. We walked past the large cathedral and then went to the beautiful modern Aarhus Museum of Art. The museum was featuring an Edvard Munch exhibition at that time, called Angst/Anxiety. It was a fantastic exhibit, including many famous paintings—Angst, The Scream and Melancholy, among others. Just the thing for a clinical psychologist to contemplate! Afterward, we went to a café overlooking the river for coffee and pastries; it was so pleasant to look at the flowing water and have a relaxed conversation.

I became very interested in doing a study at the Danish military Station Nord in Greenland, where five people are deployed for a 26-month tour. This small group lives in a highly isolated, extremely cold environment, totally alone for many months, except during the short summer when different work crews arrive for maintenance and other projects. I considered this isolated and extreme environment similar in a number of ways to the situation that a group of astronauts/cosmonauts would experience living on the surface of the moon or Mars.

Anders was not terribly enthusiastic about this idea when I first brought it up. The personnel selected for Station Nord at that time generally had different demographic characteristics than the Sirius selectees; however, I felt that the isolation and the crucial importance of working together in a safe manner would be the most important factors, and Anders came to accept this point of view. So along with considerations of the data from the Sirius Patrol research, we also started to talk about the feasibility of doing a two-year longitudinal study at Station Nord.

I wandered around Aalborg the next day, browsing in some of the shops in the old part of town near my hotel. The shops were decorated for Christmas, and there was a generally festive atmosphere, as people walked along these narrow cobblestone streets. Late in the afternoon, I came upon a small square where a group of musicians was standing at one side of the square. They were dressed in traditional festive 1900s' style coats and scarves, playing instruments and singing Christmas carols. The scene felt surreal—the snow was gently falling, the beautiful voices and the sound of trumpets and other musical instruments. I just stood there immersed, savoring the scene and the music, until they moved on to another place.

That evening, Anders, his girlfriend and I went to an Asian fusion restaurant on the waterfront for dinner. The place was full of people and very lively. The décor was quite original; throughout the area there were numerous tiny light bulbs attached to long strings hanging down from the ceiling, creating some privacy between the tables. The unique menu and the view of the fiord added to the experience. It was a wonderful evening. As I waited for my cab to the airport early the next morning, there were still many people on the streets, because the bars stay open until 5 a.m. during the holiday season. I departed on the now more familiar 6:35 a.m. flight to Amsterdam and then back home.

Station Nord, July 2014

Anders and I stayed in touch via email and Skype, as we worked out the details for the two-year longitudinal study at Station Nord. I also submitted an abstract on our Sirius research for consideration at the Humans in Space Symposium, held in Cologne in the summer of 2013. The abstract was accepted, and I suggested to Anders that he do the presentation at the conference; giving talks at scientific meetings can be a very positive professional experience, and I wanted Anders to have that chance. Besides, then I could sit back in my chair with a benign smile on my face, while a nervous someone else talked about our research! Anders did a great job and finished exactly at the required 12-minute mark. He dealt very well with questions that audience members had. After all, he had been a member of the Sirius Patrol himself. I enjoyed introducing Anders to the many attendees from the NASA Human Research Program (HRP). That evening we had dinner together with two of the women from HRP; Anders served as our German interpreter when questions came up about the menu.

Plans for the Station Nord study were moving along smoothly; this time Hans Christian Have, who was the coordinator for Station Nord and also involved in selection, was our key logistics contact in Aalborg. Working with Have, I experienced the same interest and cooperation by the Danish military as I had with the Sirius research. The plan was for Anders and me to fly to Station Nord and work directly with the group to set up the study.

Have handled the flight schedules and therefore would know when in July there would be seats available on the plane, as well as rooms in one of the barrack buildings. As it turned out, Anders decided to return to the military, with the possibility of a future one-year assignment as Sirius Patrol Chief. He continued to help with the logistics and at the same time asked his friend Jesper Corneliussen, the former Sirius Patrol member whom I had met previously, to take on a major role on the project. Now Jesper was the person I would work directly with, and he would be the one to accompany me to Station Nord.

Jesper made a good impression when I did my presentation at Aalborg University, and he was an excellent choice for continuing with the research. Jesper had his own experiences in Greenland, and he currently was a graduate student in the clinical psychology program at Aalborg University. Jesper was even taller than Anders and also from the Jutland region. I joked that I now have two Danish colleagues and friends who also are my bodyguards!

Have worked out the travel arrangements, and Jesper and I were on the roster to depart for Station Nord mid-July, from the air force base outside of Aalborg. Jesper and his family were still on their traditional Danish July holiday when I arrived in Aalborg; he had arranged for his father-in-law Peter to meet me at the airport and drive me to my hotel. That evening Peter picked me up and took me to his house for dinner. Hanne, Jesper's mother-in-law, was a fantastic cook and we had a very enjoyable time together, getting to know each other. I really appreciated all of this kindness and attention; it was pleasant to be in a local person's home. They very hospitably had invited me to stay at their house while I was in Aalborg, but I find that I am more comfortable if I stay at a hotel and not worry about disturbing people in the middle of the night, as I walk around unable to sleep well because of jet lag.

Aalborg was beginning to feel quite familiar. I made the rounds, strolling past Hotel Chagall, the trusty 7-Eleven store where they sold Cola Light and snacks, through the narrow picturesque streets with shops and cafes, over to and along the waterfront and then having a late lunch at the Restaurant Provence near the waterfront (Birgit and I had enjoyed this restaurant when we were in Aalborg together for the Sirius study).

Jesper and I worked together to compile the materials we needed to distribute to the guys at Station Nord, and he invited me to his house for dinner, the second night after their return. Jesper and his family lived on a farm outside of Aalborg. He and his wife Mette obviously had put a great deal of effort into restoring the farmhouse; their living area was an open arrangement, with great views from all sides. There also was a small outbuilding they were in the process of restoring as a "hideaway."

It was nice to meet his wife Mette and their two sons Mathias and Rasmus. I brought games and a mini-American football as presents for the boys, and University of Minnesota mugs and other souvenirs for the grown-ups. The boys were the blondest of the blond and so active. Mathias spoke a few words in English for my benefit, and he proudly showed me his butterfly and insect collections. After dinner, Mathias went into another room and, via Skype, played a board game with his cousin. That was such a good use of technology; I could hear her excited voice on the other end.

Jesper and I continued organizing the research materials, and the day before our departure, we drove to his in-law's cottage on the North Sea. The entire family was there, and after another delicious meal of fresh fish, we walked down a steep dune to the beach and the North Sea. Hanne, now retired, had been an English language teacher, and later that evening she, along with Peter, helped us with one of the translations.

Jesper drove me back to my hotel in Aalborg, and according to the plan, we were scheduled to depart the next morning for Station Nord. However, the next morning the weather was quite variable, and it wasn't clear whether or not we would be able to fly out that day (again, the reason why I always planned for several extra days for these trips). We were told to come out to the airport and just wait to see whether the weather would clear up enough to fly. I told the receptionist at the hotel that I would be back either in a week or in a few hours, I wasn't sure which. He was fine with this arrangement; Jesper picked me up and off we went.

When we got to the military airport, after a short delay we were told that the flight was a "go," and our duffel bags were loaded onto the plane. Rather than the large Hercules C-130 cargo plane, what awaited us, to the delight of those in the know, was the Queen's jet! This was a very comfortable plane, with leather seats that Queen Margrethe liked to use for her travels. We took off, and soon the crew member in charge of the roster came around to bring coffee to all the passengers. This was a great way to travel, courtesy of the Danish military. We flew straight through to Station Nord and were greeted there by many of the guys who would be our research subjects.

At Station Nord, we really were in the North; the station is located at latitude 81° 43′, only 938 km from the North Pole. The natural surroundings are quite flat and barren this far north; there are some mountains in the distance, but the station is in the tundra, and the ground is frozen close to the surface. The area around the station is covered with rocks and gravel, colored by lichen growing on the rocks.

The major feature of the station is the large gravel airstrip, and similar to Mestersvig, large enough for cargo planes to land. There was an American military presence at the station during the Cold War; along the shore, there still is a collection of oil barrels and some vehicles from that era. Station Nord also had served as an emergency landing site for U2 spy planes. The station continues to have a strategic purpose as a supply point for military stations in Greenland and in maintaining Danish sovereignty.

We walked the half-kilometer distance from the airstrip to the main part of the station; Jesper and I were assigned rooms in Building 7. The barracks had eight individual sleeping rooms, a box/trash bag toilet and shower area. A senior work crew supervisor and the chef also had rooms in the building. My room was very cozy, with bunk beds, a small desk alongside the wall and a cabinet. There were room-darkening shades on the windows, and I really couldn't ask for anything more for this incredible chance to actually be living for a few days in this very distant and unusual place.

This trip to Station Nord initiated the first year of a two-year project. Jesper and Anders had already conducted pre-deployment interviews in Denmark with the guys scheduled to arrive at Station Nord that summer. A major purpose of this trip was to go over all of the study materials with the group and have them practice the WinSCAT, a computerized cognitive assessment tool that astronauts are required to take once a month in space. First, we wanted to make sure the program was operating correctly on their individual laptops and then familiarize the guys with the program. I also did debriefing interviews with the guys who would be completing their deployment in October, to accumulate data on a larger group of participants.

Overall, we used a testing protocol that was similar to that used in the Sirius Patrol study, consisting of personality and attitude measures completed prior to deployment if possible, and at Station Nord, completion of a biweekly form that asks for ratings of mood, stress and coping and team effectiveness. The WinSCAT was scheduled on a monthly basis to examine whether there was a decline in alertness and memory over the winter darkness period.

Jesper and I met several times with the group over the next two days, while they practiced the WinSCAT to reach a baseline level of competence. Because Station Nord is too far north for the internet, the guys were given flash drives to record their data and instructed to transmit the information to Jesper in Denmark once a month via email.

The station crew lived in the main building, closest to the airstrip. The first floor had a kitchen and lounge area; the airport operations center was located on the second floor. This was the only building that was open during the winter, except for occasional visits by Sirius Patrol teams, who had their own building on the station. The center of this large, sprawling station was the *køkken*, the kitchen and dining area.

A smaller building nearby housed the bar and lounge; the deck had a fake palm tree on it, to add to the ambiance. There was a bulletin board near the entrance that was covered with business cards, mostly people from construction or maintenance companies. The photos on the wall were very interesting; all of them had been taken at the station. Prince Henrik and others were on one photo, and Queen Margrethe and a small entourage were on another. Still another photo showed a group in rather fancy, what seemed like, snowmobile suits. As I examined this photo more closely, I was surprised to see that one person in the group was a young Al Gore, the former American vice president.

Clearly, the royal family felt the importance of promoting Station Nord, the other military stations and its mission, and the Crown Prince remains actively involved in Greenland activities. (I recently heard that Queen Margrethe had been back to Daneborg and had helped out in the kitchen after dinner. Now there is an egalitarian role model!)

The station was quite busy; during our stay, there were workers from Denmark and Iceland, two indigenous men from a village in Greenland and four Danish soldiers on assignment. There were several fun traditions at the station that Jesper and I were fortunate enough to be part of. Saturday night is a special time, and there is a tradition for everyone to dress up and wear a tie. In fact, there is a bulletin board in the dining room featuring ties and the name of the wearer pinned on to it. Jesper used his ingenuity and made his own tie out of wood and painted it red. Certainly the epitome of polar fashion, and the tie may still be on the wall to this day, who knows? (I did see it still up there on my return trip in 2016). So that I would be in the spirit of the evening, one of the construction men lent me a tie.

There was a special meal that evening, and then everyone headed over to the bar. Sunday was a rest day for everyone; people could sleep in as long as they wanted to and go over to the kitchen at any time to help themselves to breakfast and leftovers.

The bar was an amazing experience. It was just so much fun! I was the only woman on the entire station, and the guys kept asking me to join in with their activities. One game is apparently a traditional Danish pub game. A large tree stump is placed in the middle of the room, with a nail pounded in up to about 1 mm or so from the surface. The game is to slam the nail with a hammer but not hard enough to completely pound the nail in. The one who pounds the nail closest to the stump surface without contacting the surface is the winner.

The guys kept asking me to take a turn, but these are construction guys and certainly more used to wielding a hammer than I was. I demurred and just cheered them on. The other big activity was drinking down shots of some fiery Danish liquor, as fast as you can. I tried a shot of this liquor and quickly decided that it was in my best interest to stick to beer.

It is strange to be walking over to your sleeping quarters when the sun is brightly shining, the sky is a clear blue and it is eleven o'clock at night. But the room-darkening shades do help. The next morning, at some point I went over to the *køkken* for breakfast. I found the chef fast asleep, with some colored lines all over his face. As a prank, some of the guys painted magic marker lines on his face while he was sleeping, and the question was how long it would take before he would notice it (he was not too happy when he saw his face in a mirror later in the day). Jesper and I, in the early afternoon, straightened up the bar area and we got to work in this now very quiet building.

The construction crews at the station were working hard to finish several building and maintenance projects during the short summer period. A new building was going up in the area where the incinerator was located. Also, there was an almost-finished Aarhus University research building going up a bit away from the center of the station; some of the research equipment had already been flown in. The Station Nord guys were busy with maintenance projects in addition to their duties in the observation tower. I was occupied doing debriefing interviews with the departing group, trying to coordinate schedules with everything else that was going on at the same time.

Mealtimes were a new experience. There always was a wide array of food—several appetizers, two main dishes, bread, pastries and desserts. I was bemused watching the traditional Scandinavian way of going through a buffet line. First a slice of bread, then spoonsful of food spread on top and other foods neatly added to the side of the plate. My usual buffet behavior was just to pile the food on!

The conversation at the table sometimes turned to the work one of us was doing. Jesper and I were having some trouble getting the WinSCAT to work properly; fortunately, I was able to get emails through to our contact person at NASA for some troubleshooting. The others we were eating with were very interested in hearing about our progress and the messages with NASA, just as we asked them how they were doing when one of them shared some glitch in their work. All of us were equal; Jesper and I were just two of the workers at the station.

It was good when I had a bit of time to wander around the station, although I did not wander too far away because of the ever-present threat of polar bears. One afternoon, Poul, one of the station guys, walked with me to explore some of the very old original wooden buildings on the perimeter of the station. These buildings are still standing because of the asbestos in them and the difficulty in decontaminating them in this isolated environment.

One of the buildings contained the radio communication equipment used during the 1950s. I particularly wanted to see this building and its equipment because Torben, who got me involved with Greenland in the first place, had worked here as a radio operator during the Cold War. I took a few photos in this dark and dusty "museum," which I sent to Torben when I returned.

Jesper was having a wonderful time bonding with the guys and having a reunion with his friend Michael, a former member of the Sirius Patrol (Greenland is a small world). I was really delighted to see Michael again. He had been one of the "new guys" in our Sirius Patrol study, and both Birgit and I had spent a lot of time talking with him after we had completed the interviews.

One evening at around 10 p.m., Jesper and Michael packed a radio and a firearm, took along the two pet dogs at the station and walked out of the station to hike to an area a few kilometers away. It was a beautiful night, and I simply sat on a bench in front of the *køkken* and just hung out, totally relaxed and happy. Another spectacular night, I went to bed but I realized there was no way I would be able to fall asleep just then. The only solution was to get dressed and walk over to join the group still schmoozing in the bar.

Those chosen for Station Nord were required to be skilled in English in order to communicate with pilots flying in the vicinity. This was very helpful, because I was able to do the debriefing interviews in English and not have another person involved to translate. On our fourth day at the station, the station chief suddenly came running into my room during an interview and told me that Jesper and I were flying out in a few hours! He said that the plane would be on the ground for about 1.5 hours; this gave me enough time to do a short debriefing interview with the guy who was returning after a period back in Denmark.

This individual had been dealing with personal issues related to his girlfriend breaking up with him, and he needed direct professional help to cope with this problem. Fortunately, both he and his therapist judged that he now had the psychological strengths to resume his duties at Station Nord (as with the Sirius Patrol findings, relationship problems at home were taking a toll on the psychological status and performance of personnel in a long-duration isolated environment).

Too bad to be leaving so soon. Four days at Station Nord just weren't enough. Tommy, one of the station guys, drove up to my barracks in an ATV, picked up my duffel bag and took it over to the plane; he then drove the returning guy from the plane to my room. We were about halfway through the interview when someone else came rushing in and asked me to hurry up because the plane was leaving very soon and I had to get over there right away (it certainly is not a good way to do an interview, but there are circumstances that one simply does not have control over, interview or not).

I started walking/running as fast as I could to get to the plane when Tommy, my knight on an ATV, came roaring over. I hopped on the vehicle, grabbed onto him and both of us, laughing, raced to the plane. This was my first view of this huge C-130 Hercules cargo plane, and it really is gigantic. There was still time to take some pictures—me, laptop in a case hanging from a shoulder strap, standing in front of the plane with Royal Danish Air Force painted on its side. One of the guys also took a few shots of me with the other people who were leaving at the same time.

For sure, one needs to be flexible in this environment with changing weather and schedules. We were told that we were going to fly to Keflavik Military Airport in Iceland, adjacent to the main airport, stay overnight in Keflavik and then go on to Aalborg the next day. Whatever!!! I was delighted to have another time, even though short, in Iceland.

Flying on a Hercules cargo plane is a rather different experience than flying Delta Airlines. The interior of the plane was full of cargo, lashed down with webbing and straps. Rows of metal benches were set up in the front area, parallel to the side of the plane; the benches had blankets on them for cushioning. There was a rather elaborate seat belt with a shoulder strap which Jesper helped me with; it stood in good stead as the plane took off and we started to ascend. Since we were facing the side rather than the front of the plane, the seat belts held us from sliding sideways on the seat. It was possible to lean back against the webbing hanging down from the sides of the plane, and this was quite comfortable. Headphones were a necessity because of the loud noise from the plane's engines, so it was not possible to converse with anyone. But Jesper offered me some snacks and off we went.

The toilet was an interesting experience. It was located about halfway toward the back of the plane. I was very careful walking back there to avoid tripping over the metal runners and other obstacles along the floor. There was a small ramp that one had to walk up and then get past a curtain, behind which was the toilet (a box setup). This felt a bit precarious because the box was on a small flat area very close to the edge of the ramp. But this was just another adventure! When I returned to my seat, Jesper was watching a film with subtitles on his laptop. I leaned over, he moved his laptop so we both could see and we spent part of the flight, heads together, watching a movie. What a nice friend!

It was late in the evening when we got to our hotel in Keflavik. Two of the men on the plane who had been to Station Nord on construction business joined Jesper and me as we wandered down the street looking for a restaurant that was still open. We found an Asian restaurant that was still serving, and afterward we decided to stop for a beer at a nearby pub. (The ever-present light at this time of year is so invigorating; none of us were particularly tired.) We settled in with our beers and then one very drunk man seemed to take a fancy to me. (You've got to be kidding!) He kept coming over to our table and talking to me. I tried to ignore him, but to no avail.

When we left the pub, he followed us and this time it was harassment rather than talk. I simply looped my arm through the arm of one of my walking companions and told the guy that my husband did not like his intentions. I'm not sure how this got through the language barrier, but it worked and he stopped following us. Anyway, I had my Jaeger Corps/Sirius buddy/bodyguard Jesper right alongside. But this was surely an unexpected experience!

We got back to Aalborg the next day without delay. I had plans to take the train the following morning to Odense to interview Christian, a Sirius Patrol friend of Anders and Jesper who had successfully completed a solo sailing voyage circumnavigating the world. Anders had asked him whether he wanted to be part of our research program; Christian agreed and followed the study protocol for the entire duration of his voyage. I was keen to meet him and do a debriefing interview.

Because of construction on the train line, I had to take a bus from Aalborg to a nearby town and then connect to the train to Odense. Christian met me the next morning at my hotel. I've discovered that during the day, hotel bars are excellent places for a quiet conversation—there is usually no one else in the room. So, indeed, we went into the bar, and before I knew it, we had talked for over three hours!!! I began with the interview questions about his voyage, but then our conversation turned to many other topics, including Christian's still unsettled plans for the future in terms of work, marriage, children and his interest in my career and the research I had been doing over the years.

Eventually, Christian realized what time it was and that he had to get to his job as harbor master. He asked one of the people working at the hotel to come over and take a picture of the two of us. That was such a nice gesture. He then gave me a big hug and left for work. Christian is a lovely person, bright, friendly and the same as so many of the expeditioners I have met with over the years. These men and women have a period in their lives when they march to the beat of their own drummer, taking delight in their independence and their love of nature.

I stayed over that night to have a chance to see more of Odense. The old part of the city has the same charm that I've seen in other cities and towns in Denmark. Colorfully painted houses, narrow cobblestone streets, restaurants with plants and ironware decorations hanging from the upper windows. At the large square near my hotel, I was bemused to see a young couple lounging on a massive sculpture of reclining male and female figures.

Odense is the birthplace of Hans Christian Andersen. I did a tour through his childhood home and the adjacent museum, and I just walked around taking in the sights of the city. I did find a great traditional restaurant, where I scored big and enjoyed a three-herring lunch!!!

I returned for a last evening in Aalborg, said goodbye to Jesper and thanked him heartily for all of his help and friendship. The next day, I took the early morning flight to Amsterdam and back home. At Schipol Airport, I got upgraded to first class for the flight to Minneapolis. This was really amusing, considering that on my last flight I was sitting on a metal bench on a cargo plane. So I couldn't resist—I stood in the aisle and took a picture of my posh seat, and then settled in to be pampered on the 8-hour flight home.

Station Nord, July 2016

Over the two-year period of the study, we accumulated a large dataset on 10 people. The Station Nord guys were cooperating extremely well. Jesper kept in contact with Anders and retrieved and coded the monthly data sent from Station Nord. I felt that the findings from our research would be informative in providing insights on the questions posed by the research—the psychological and work performance effects of living and working in an isolated, confined and extreme environment for an extended duration while experiencing the extreme range of light/dark cycles.

Anders was now in Daneborg, serving as Sirius Patrol Chief. Jesper was unable to accompany me during this July summer period because of family responsibilities; however, he arranged for Marie Troelsgaard, one of his fellow psychology graduate students, to come with me to Station Nord and help out with the interviews and data coding. The debriefing interviews were the final step of our two-year longitudinal project.

I met briefly with Marie at my hotel in Aalborg, and we talked about some of the realities of life at Station Nord and the upcoming research tasks. The following day, Jesper and I went to the university to photocopy the materials I would be taking to Station Nord. Late afternoon, along with Marie, we went to Jesper and Mette's house to work on the study forms and have dinner there. It was really nice to see how much their boys had grown in the two years since my last visit and to see the new remodeling done to an outbuilding near their main house. We also got to see the boys feeding their pet goats.

There was a several-day delay in departing for Station Nord because of poor weather in Greenland; finally, the flight schedules were cleared, and Jesper drove us to the military airport for our morning flight. This time, we flew from Aalborg in a Hercules cargo plane, with a planned stop at Keflavik. The passengers on this flight included the six Sirius Patrol "new guys" and a cook heading for Mestersvig Station. She would be connecting in Keflavik to another flight to Mestersvig that the Sirius guys would be on as well.

People onboard or in the military terminal in Keflavik often looked at me quizzically or with amusement, wondering what on earth I would be doing in Greenland. There was a woman pilot on the plane, apparently connecting in Keflavik for her own flight. Because of the airplane noise and everyone wearing headphones, it really wasn't possible to talk with her; however, I showed her the slides on my laptop from Anders's presentation in Cologne.

When we arrived in Keflavik, we were told that the weather in Greenland was not good, and a decision was made that everyone would stay overnight in Iceland. Hotel arrangements in Reykjavik were taken care of for all of us on the plane; everyone seemed delighted to have this chance to spend some time in Reykjavik. For the Sirius guys, this would be their last time in "civilization" before their 26-month deployment in Greenland. Marie and I were housed at a hotel with a seafaring motif, close to the water; we found a restaurant that served fresh lobster and spent the evening walking around, taking pictures and just enjoying the beautiful city we unexpectedly ended up in.

We all had contingency plans to rent a car and tour the Golden Triangle the next day, depending on which of us, if any, would fly out the following day. I invited the cook to join us if all of us remained. The next morning, a bus came by the hotels and we were taken back to the airport. The Sirius guys were a bit the worse for wear after their last night out! As it turned out, the weather was better at Station Nord than Mestersvig, so Marie and I departed and the others had a day to do some sightseeing.

It felt really good to be going back to Station Nord and complete a study that had extended over a considerable period of time. The guys were very happy to meet Marie and have a woman closer to their own age on the station. For me, it was a reunion with the three guys who had been new arrivals in 2014; I also enjoyed meeting for the first time the two guys in our study who arrived in 2015 and the three newly arrived guys who were just starting their deployment at Station Nord. Building 7 was again my home, as well as Marie's. There were other researchers at the station—four Canadians who had a contract with NASA to fly over Arctic areas to survey the thickness of the ice. Mohammed (Mo), one of the pilots, had a room across from me (actually my 2014 room); the woman scientist and two others were in another building. There also was a construction crew from Iceland at the station and several others from Denmark, also involved in various construction/maintenance projects.

Rune, the station chief, had set up a tentative schedule for the debriefing interviews beginning the next morning. Station Nord covers a large area, so whenever I was finished with one interview, that guy radioed the next guy on the schedule to come to my room for his interview. This usually involved someone roaring up on an ATV. Marie helped with one of the interviews with a guy whose English skills were not as good as the others.

I wanted to complete all of the interviews and collect the last questionnaire data as soon as possible, having had the experience in 2014 when there was a sudden change in the flight schedule and we had to depart in a hurry. We finished all of the interviews and received the completed questionnaires over a two-day period. Marie and I worked on the data, but for the most part, we were now free to enjoy being at Station Nord.

I relished the opportunity to truly get a feel for the life of the station. Each morning, often accompanied by Marie, I took long walks exploring different parts of the station area, but not too far, remembering the polar bear warnings. I stopped to check out the different work projects and took lots of pictures. I really wanted to remember this place. The Icelandic crew was assembling and welding together components of a large oil storage tank that was several stories high; others in a different area of the station were driving heavy equipment and clearing the ground. Marie and I became friendly with one of the Icelandic guys, and he asked us if we wanted to check out the storage tank he was working on. We walked in, and it looked even bigger from the inside. Continuing with our walk, we noted one building not too far away from this site that was the Sirius Patrol storage area. The teams slept inside when they were passing through on their journeys and also at times during the summer when they were laying in supplies. Marie and I took pictures of each other in front of the massive snow plows. The blades alone were almost at my shoulder height. There was a door that opened to the engine area; it was actually possible to walk inside and around the engine.

I chatted a lot with the Canadians and particularly with Mo, who was just across the hall from me, so we were practically roommates. They were quite frustrated with the weather conditions because it kept them from their surveillance tasks. The weather had to be clear in Svalbard as an emergency landing place before they could receive permission for a flight. Marie and I walked over to their plane with them a few times to check out their monitoring equipment and, just in general, to share some time together.

Lunch times became quite amusing. The area in front of the *køkken* became a parking lot! The construction guys would drive up for lunch in their huge vehicles from the distant parts of the station where they were working. On the floor of the entry area to the *køkken*, there were several boxes with blown-up bags of snack foods. The story was that a supply plane from Ukraine that the Danish military contracts with flew in a shipment that included these various foods; however, they did not load these boxes in a pressurized area, and all of the bags burst, along with some glass panes they were bringing in. So, whoever wanted exploded corn puffs or chips, they were free for the taking!

The *køkken* area generally was a pleasant place to be around; there were benches out front just to sit and relax for a bit. The dog on the station usually stood outside an open kitchen window, his head inside to smell the aroma and watch the cooks preparing the food.

The three new station guys were very interested in hearing about the research project and my other research. Since we were completing the data collection with this visit, these new guys would not be involved. However, they were so enthusiastic about the idea of a research project that I offered to do the pre-deployment interviews with each of them. With their permission, I shared the information with Kent, head of Stations and Patrol Service Greenland, when I returned to Aalborg. They really were the new guys, still in a learning process and getting comfortable with their responsibilities. They definitely became our pals over the rest of our stay at the station.

Anders was now at Daneborg, overseeing the summer work before the start of the Sirius Patrol Fall journeys. He called Rune, the station chief, and they arranged a time when Anders would call back so I could talk with him. Mads, one of the new guys, was in the observation room at the time; he handed me some notes to pass on to Anders with some recommendations about their previous training experiences.

One day Jesper L., another of the new guys, asked me if I wanted to ride with him to a reservoir at the edge of the station to pump water. It was a totally new experience for me to be riding in this huge truck; I had to climb up several steps to get into the cab. Afterward, Mads invited Marie and me to a hotdog roast. There was a problem with the incinerator, so Mads and Jesper L. were tasked with burning a large amount of trash on the shore; this was in the area that was full of 1950s' leftovers and oil cans. They got this huge fire going, and Mads used something for a shield and stuck a hot dog on a very long stick near the edge of the fire. This was rather impressive considering the size of the fire! Next, Poul entered the scene. He had just completed one year at the station, so he now was a veteran.

Poul brought along a rifle for target practice and a flare gun. He clearly was an expert shot; whatever Mads threw into the air, Poul was right on target to hit it. Now our new best friend Poul urged Marie and me to take a turn at target practice. Marie obliged, but I just couldn't get myself to shoot a rifle. It was not realistic, but I had this fear that I would shoot someone by mistake! However, I did oblige to shoot off a non-lethal flare with the other gun.

I increasingly enjoyed the scenery and the station with each passing day. Although the first impression of Station Nord is one of barrenness, there is the sun shining on the water, the small Arctic flowers, and despite all of the activity, I had a real feeling of peace and wonder to actually be at this place so far from outside civilization. Each of these days at the station was another chance to soak in the views and get some exercise.

One day while walking back for lunch, I had another bonding experience. I heard an increasingly loud noise behind me and saw a vehicle similar to a golf cart with four of the Icelandic crew in heavy work overalls squeezed into it. The driver stopped and offered me a ride; I said "sure," so the guy next to the driver moved over, I hopped on and I rode back to the *køkken* in style.

The big event, of course, was the Saturday evening festivities. The station that season had two Danish Navy chefs, and they were really good. They made menus listing all of the food that was served and baked a very fancy dessert with an anchor in chocolate frosting on the side of the plate. Everyone went over to the bar afterward, and while the tree stump was no longer there, there were plenty of other activities going on. A major event was a timed drinking contest. I certainly had experience slamming down shots from my Russian travel days; however, I very prudently decided not to get into this contest, even though the guys were impressed with how fast I had downed a small shot of their very strong liquor.

After a while, I went out to the deck; it was a totally international group, all having a great time—lots of laughter and kidding around. As the evening progressed, two of the Icelanders got into an arm-wrestling contest. They were strong husky guys! The contest went on for quite a while, and, unfortunately, one of the Icelanders suffered a broken bone in his hand. Oh! This was not good, and everyone felt really bad about this.

On Sunday, the next morning, I was in my room scoring some of the questionnaires when Marie came in to tell me that I had an email message. My daughter Michelle had sent me an email via Jesper in Denmark that my favorite cousin had died. This was quite a shock, and it took me a long time to get over the disbelief about his passing. Here I was in an isolated place in the far north of Greenland; I needed to deal with my feelings of grief in this isolation. The recognition of how far I was from home really had an impact.

But time moves on. A plane flew in the following day to take the injured guy back to Iceland to get the bone set. It wasn't clear whether he would be able to return to the station to resume his job, but a few days later, a small jet flew in and our guy was back! He was greeted heartily, as was the pilot. When the pilot left, he circled the station, wagged his wings and then flew off. What a feeling of community spirit, from the people on the ground welcoming their buddy to the pilot in the air. And I thought about how nice it was to be schmoozing with Icelanders, pilots and the many others who in my usual walk of life I likely never would have had contact with.

More exploring with the station guys. Poul showed Marie and me the building where he did his carpentry work and also two cages holding his pet lemmings. I asked him what they did for entertainment in the winter, and he said that the major entertainment was going out on the runway and shooting lemmings. He said that he was very happy to have been a part of the research and he asked me whether I would do a talk for the Station Nord crew at their living quarters. I was very happy to do so.

Ever the ready professor, I prepared some slides and that evening I told them about the psychological work that NASA was doing, and how the study they had participated in was designed to answer some of the questions about supporting astronauts on long-duration missions. I showed them some slide photos from the last Discovery shuttle flight that I had attended; I had been given a VIP invitation, so I was able to sit up close and have a very good view of the launchpad across the lake from the bleachers. I told them how exciting it was to actually be there, hear the noise and experience the vibrations of the liftoff and see the rocket with the attached shuttle slowly ascend.

All of these guys were just so nice! Certain facts are not secret because the flight roster with everyone's birthdate and passport information is simply sitting on a shelf in the operations tower. The guys thought it was really something that at my age I was still flying around the world and hanging out in Greenland. I stayed in contact with the guys when I returned home and sent them holiday greetings. In response, they sent me a photo of themselves dressed up in different funny costumes. (From Danish fairy tales, maybe?)

Poul was in charge of the souvenir shop at the station. I already had a T-shirt and some small souvenirs from my last visit, but he insisted that I take back additional things from this trip, courtesy of the station. He kept handing me more and more objects; I didn't feel comfortable taking all of this, but it felt like I would be hurting his feelings if I did not agree. He also gave Marie some souvenirs to take back. This was true largesse.

Station Nord really grew on me during the five days we were there, and I felt very sad to leave, knowing I would never see this place again. Mads rather plaintively had asked me, "Gloria, will you come back again next summer?" But our project was finished. (Actually, I would go back in a heartbeat if I ever had another opportunity; the same for Daneborg. I still visualize my morning and late afternoon walks around the station, and how special it felt.)

We knew an approximate time when the plane would arrive to take us back to Aalborg. Some of the guys lined up on the roof of their building to take pictures of the plane landing. It did arrive on time, and it kind of took my breath away to see this huge plane touch ground with dust streaming behind it, ride across the large gravel landing strip and finally come to a stop.

The flight back to Aalborg was "relatively" uneventful. There were some concerns about the weather down the line, but we took off with the caveat that if the weather was bad in Aalborg when we landed for refueling in Keflavik, we would return to Station Nord. There is an advantage of sitting on a bench and being able to stretch out without a row of seats in front of you. Over the course of the flight, one of the pilots brought out coffee and several people wandered in and out of the cockpit area. Of course, I decided to have a look; I walked up the steps to the cockpit, and the pilots greeted me with smiles and offered me some coffee. A young daughter of one of the pilots was sitting in a high alcove toward the back of the cockpit, reading a book.

It was quite an experience to be standing in this large cockpit, looking at all of the controls and the view out the window. Certainly not the experience a passenger would have on a commercial airline. We landed at Keflavik, disembarked and went through security screening. There still was a delay because of the weather and lots of discussion back and forth whether we would return to Station Nord or continue on to Aalborg. Eventually, we flew on to Aalborg and was greeted there by Jesper, Kent and the local crew.

That evening, Jesper, Marie and I went for dinner together, after which I said goodbye to Marie. I had planned for extra days to take the train up to Skagen, which is on the North Sea at the northernmost point in Denmark and a favorite tourist spot because of the beautiful sand dunes and large marina. It was truly a day well spent. My last day in Aalborg was a sentimental walk past all of the places that had become so familiar over these Greenland times. I found a book store that had Hans Christen Andersen fairy tales in English, and I bought copies for my grandchildren. Jesper and I had a special farewell dinner that evening at the Fisk and Skaldyr restaurant, and I departed the next morning on the 6:35 a.m. flight.

When I got back home with all of the data in my carry-on that I had just collected, Birgit, my friend and colleague from Daneborg, worked with me to organize the entire complicated two-year dataset. She did an amazing job putting together all of the material from different people coming to the station at different deployment times and putting all of it in a format for conducting the statistical analyses.

The study results were very interesting. A major theme that emerged centered on conflict resolution. In any group, and particularly a small group that must live and work together in isolated and confined conditions, conflicts can escalate, destroy the cohesion of the group and have detrimental effects on their work performance. Some of the comments during the interviews showed the importance of the leader listening to all points of view when a difference of opinion occurred but then asserting authority and making the final decision. Other comments demonstrated the dilemmas that can occur during conflict situations—deciding whether to "pick sides" and intervene during an argument or just let the argument run its course. The consensus was that the best approach was to stay out of the conflict and let it get resolved by other means, if that was at all possible.

The importance of conflict resolution highlighted by this and other studies has direct application for space missions. Several of the astronauts have commented that it is not the fact of having a difference of opinion or a more heated exchange, because it is inevitable that disagreements will happen over time. The important issue is how these differences are resolved.

The cognitive battery of tests that examined the effects of darkness on alertness and concentration showed that people were simply different. Despite some of the scientific findings in the literature, our study showed that some of the group actually performed better during the darkness period, others showed no difference and a few performed somewhat worse. This factor of individual differences is, for me, an area of great interest. It sometimes is an error to make generalizations about people as a single entity; finding out what makes them different is the challenge.

We also studied the personal values of the group by means of a questionnaire administered before and after, or toward the end of their time at the station. We found that the values of benevolence (an interest and concern for others) and self-direction (independence) had high ratings among the group and remained high over the period of their deployment. These personal values seem to be highly compatible for positive adaptation and work in an isolated environment over a long period of time.

In my advisory committee work with NASA, I have used the findings from this and other studies to recommend that the NASA Human Research Program (HRP) provide specific training in conflict resolution to astronauts and others involved in the space program. A current HRP project that I am a part of will study American and Russian subjects living for eight months in a Mars simulation habitat in Moscow. We will continue to evaluate this issue of conflict resolution, based on the self-report and behavioral observations of the participants.

21

EXPEDITION ICE MAIDENS

England, October 2018

In 2018, I received an email message from a clinical psychologist in the UK who worked for the British military, asking whether I had an interest in collaborating on a study of a team of six military women who were training to traverse the Antarctic continent. She indicated that the purpose of the study was to promote the ability of women in the military service to work together to attain a significant arduous goal and to study biological processes—thermal regulation in the severe cold, hormonal functioning and psychological, group process factors. I was delighted about the possibility of collaborating on this project. The last studies that I had carried out were on all-men groups, and I actually had been asking the two women expeditioners I had studied many years previously to let me know if they heard of any women teams.

The British six-woman team was formed through a rigorous down-selection sequence that included observations of applicants' physical and behavioral performance over three expedition training periods in the UK and Arctic areas of Norway, winnowing down from an initial pool of over 250 volunteers to the six chosen in the final phase. The expedition, named Exercise Ice Maidens by the poetic Brits, consisted of five officers and one noncommissioned officer. Two of the women, including the team leader, were primary care physicians; several had multiple deployments in Afghanistan, Iraq and Kosovo.

With the help of emails, Skype and phone calls, I worked with Rachel Norris, the psychologist who initially had contacted me, and Jodie Blackadder-Weinstein, a primary care physician and squadron leader in the British Royal Air Force. Jodie was my primary collaborator on the psychological component of the research. Our initial contacts focused on the application that had to be submitted to the Ministry of Defence Research Ethics Committee for approval to conduct the research.

The psychological component of the application required extensive details about how informed consent would be obtained from the participants, study procedures, specific questionnaires and interview materials chosen, and the rationale for the selection of these specific research instruments. This was quite a laborious process, but Jodie, Rachel and I worked together along with some others, and approval for the research was granted.

Jodie organized the method for collecting data in Antarctica. Each of the team members was given a smartphone with a rating form loaded on it; they were instructed to complete the form once a week, save it on their phone and download the data when they returned from Antarctica. I planned to travel to England as soon as possible after the team returned to do the debriefing interviews. The timing of the interviews is very important—memories can get distorted when people are away from the actual situation; media attention and other factors also can have an influence on the recall of an event. I always find the personal interviews to be highly informative in clarifying the meaning of the scores obtained on questionnaires. And very important, I totally enjoy meeting with expeditioners, and in the case of these women, I envied their opportunity to experience this adventure.

The expedition proceeded on schedule, and the team, pulling sleds with all of their gear, reached their goal of traversing the Antarctic continent in 61 days, covering 1,700 km. Upon their return, a date was set for the team to gather at the prestigious Royal Military Academy at Sandhurst to do the debriefing interviews; also, the several other researchers conducting studies on the team would carry out their several biological tests.

Jodie worked out the logistics for my stay. This time on expedition research, I arrived in style on a direct flight to London on Delta Airlines. Jodie met me at Heathrow Airport, and we drove to a town near Sandhurst for lunch. It was great to finally meet her in person, and there was no problem finding a lot to talk about. She took me to the hotel that was arranged for my stay. I was rather astonished to see where they were putting me up! Frimley Hall and Spa in Camberley is a large, stately and very impressive Victorian manor house, with beautiful surrounding grounds and, as I found out, a gourmet, very formal restaurant. This really felt like British aristocracy!

Jodie drove several hours back to her home in Birmingham, and the next day, which was a Sunday, she drove back and very pleasantly served as my tour guide. Our first stop was Windsor Castle, which was nearby. The town of Windsor was full of people and the shops all had different souvenir memorabilia for the upcoming royal marriage of Prince Harry and

Meghan Markle. We stopped for tea, and similar to my usual experience when I am in a foreign country, it was interesting to see and hear people with different accents and languages, view the architecture and get a bit of a feel for a way of life. I also had to get used to seeing cars and buses driving on the left side of the road while I was crossing; it was rather terrifying the first few times.

We did a tour of Windsor Castle. Jodie told me that this was her first time inside the castle, so it was a nice experience for both of us. Walking through the courtyard, I noticed the closed door to St. George's Chapel, where the upcoming royal marriage ceremony would take place. We topped off the day together in a very special way. Jodie had made a reservation for afternoon tea at the stately Cliveden House estate, a large and majestic building and grounds that was the scene of the Profumo scandal in the 1960s, which involved the resignation of the secretary of state for war, who was involved in a rather dangerous sexual affair.

We walked into the lobby. My first impression was seeing the beautiful fireplace and the very luxurious décor. An older gentleman in very formal clothing ushered us into another room and seated us at a small table. A server soon approached and asked me what kind of tea I wanted to order. It was almost intimidating—I didn't have a clue! I asked Jodie to choose, and she ordered several arrays. This was my first experience of a tea and crumpets traditional event; the crumpets were served on a three-tier serving tray along with tiny cucumber sandwiches and small pastries, all arranged in ascending order. This day was indeed a very memorable prelude to the post-expedition research.

Jodie stayed nearby at her in-law's house, and we spent part of the next day going over the expedition data and meeting some of the other investigators. I was very impressed with the breadth of the biological research that had been carried out on this group of women. The different studies measured metabolic processes of interest and their changes over time from the pre- to the post-expedition period. Over the course of the trek, the focus was on the physiological adaptation of a highly fit group of women during an extended period of physical exertion in the extreme cold. Heart rate, body temperature and other parameters were monitored by innovatively designed biosensors that were sewn into the bras of the team members.

The endocrinologist involved in the research had a laboratory in one of the far buildings at Sandhurst. Jodie and I drove to the building to see his laboratory setup and hear about his work. His expedition research included the study of cold adaptation before and after the trek; he had flown to

Chile to carry out his evaluations of the team as soon as possible after they left the ice. I shared with Jodie and him some of the thermoregulation findings from the space suit research I had been part of, as a comparison.

I also met Mike Smith, whom Jodie described as "her boss." When I was introduced to him, he was carrying a large shopping bag that contained 12 bras, two from each expeditioner. These were the bras with the biosensors sewn into them, and they couldn't be washed until the sensors were removed. So, another perspective on doing biological research!

That evening, I had a chance to meet Rachel and the others who had studied in the team at a dinner at an Indian restaurant. In contrast to the informal Danes, the people I met kept addressing me as "Professor Leon"; however, I quickly asked them to call me "Gloria," and then we were able to chat in a more relaxed way. During our meal, one of the physician expedition women who knew some of the investigators dropped by to say hello.

The next day was set aside for the interviews and then a drive to London to stay overnight there. The entrance to the main building at Sandhurst where I would conduct the interviews was another impressive experience. History and tradition were everywhere. In the large main corridor, there were many photos on the walls dating back several centuries; each pillar had the name of a country chiseled into the wall and beneath, a photo of military officers in full dress uniforms. The countries were formerly part of the British Empire—India, Egypt and Libya.

The room where I did the interviews had a large table; all of the chair backs had the Queen's royal cypher on them: EIIR. There were two huge fireplaces on one wall, and alongside each, a cheetah skin. Ouch!! Rachel had arrived earlier and came in to say hello. I was introduced to Rebecca, who, like Jodie, is a military primary care physician. Rebecca recorded the interviews and served as scribe, typing the responses to each of the interview questions.

I was really looking forward to meeting the expeditioners. I had seen photographs of the team from media coverage of their departure to Antarctica and had read some of their blog comments posted during the expedition. Contrary to some stereotypes that expeditioners need to be big and brawny to ski and pull heavy loaded sleds over difficult terrain, the women I met with came in all shapes and sizes. Several were relatively small in stature and of medium body build, others were taller and had more prominent body mass (as with the men, their success was related to training and endurance, not brute strength). One of the women mentioned during the interview that when they had reached their goal, she felt that she just could have kept on skiing. According to tradition, the men are referred to as "the boys" and the women as "the girls," but there was no way I could call this accomplished group of women "the girls."

I brought along small NASA souvenirs for each of the women—pens and a sticker with the motto, "Never Give Up." I thought this was an appropriate statement for a group that so recently had accomplished a very notable success. Most of the women seemed quite relaxed talking with me once we got past the first interview question; although they smiled about amusing things that had happened during the expedition, they also talked about difficult situations they had encountered.

All of the expeditioners except one appeared for their interview in informal athletic clothing. The exception was the woman who had served in the military for the longest period of time, compared to the others. She appeared rather tense during the first part of the interview, perhaps related to physical problems she had experienced during the trek that caused some difficulties.

It was a long but very interesting day doing all six interviews. I also was introduced to and had a short conversation with the professor who developed the biosensors used in the study. He would not be at his Centre in London the next day when Jodie and I were scheduled to tour the facility, so we had a quick chat during which he expressed an interest in testing out his sensors in space suit garments (I set up a contact between this professor and my space suit colleagues at the University of North Dakota when I returned).

Toward the end of the afternoon, I felt some time pressure doing the interviews, but we finished up with everyone having their say, and then we got ready for the drive to London. Rebecca, who had worked hard all through the day typing the interview comments, accompanied Jodie, who did the driving, and me to London. We drove directly to the restaurant to have dinner with Air Commodore Rich Withnall, who was the medical director of the Royal Centre for Defense Medicine in Birmingham, the department Jodie was part of.

Rich was in London for a conference, and this was a nice opportunity to meet the person who was the overall head of the expedition research. He was very friendly and informal, and I had fun telling the group about some of my crazy Russian experiences. I had joked with Jodie the day before that I thought the Commodore title sounded like he could be the captain of the Love Boat television series. She said that I should tell him that, but of course I didn't.

At dinner, I mentioned again the suggestion I had brought up earlier with the other researchers, that we include all of our individual scientific papers on our expedition findings into a single published volume. We had a unique dataset on women in extreme environments that would certainly be of overall scientific interest. Unfortunately, however, it never happened.

Another upscale hotel was arranged for me while Jodie stayed elsewhere. I told Jodie that I felt uncomfortable that she was staying in a "lesser" place, but she diplomatically said that the arrangements were just fine. Our plan for the next morning was to visit the Imperial College of London and tour the Hamlyn Centre headed by the professor I had met the previous day.

As we walked into the Centre complex, my attention was drawn to a large photograph of Queen Elizabeth; she had personally dedicated the Centre a few years previously. Two of the research assistants showed us around the research laboratories and told us more about the innovative technologies invented there, including the biosensors the team wore during the expedition. The laboratory group was really on top of things; they already were in the process of writing a scientific paper on their expedition findings. Jodie and I also were impressed with the robotic devices that had been developed for surgery and other devices they still were working on.

Afterward, we had lunch at a Mediterranean restaurant near the College. It was interesting to see the many students in the place and lots of activity. We spent about an hour at the nearby Museum of Natural History and then headed out of London toward Birmingham, Jodie's home, and where I would spend three nights at my friend Judith Fisher's house. Jodie drove past Buckingham Palace and other sights on the way to the highway, so I could see some of the London landmarks.

Traffic getting out of London was very heavy. It took longer that she expected to arrive in Birmingham at Judith and her husband Anthony George's house, where both Jodie and I were invited for dinner. Judith was a retired physician and had been very active in the World Association for Disaster and Emergency Medicine (WADEM). We met through that association and developed a long-standing friendship and professional relationship. I was very happy to see her again and meet Anthony for the first time.

Jodie and I planned to meet in two days' time to continue working on the data coding and initial analyses. In the meantime, the following day Judith and Anthony took me to Stratford-upon-Avon for lunch and a matinee performance of Twelfth Night at the Royal Shakespeare Theatre. This was really a very special treat, and I was so grateful to have this experience.

Judith and I spent some very good time catching up on our lives and doing a bit of sightseeing. Since Jodie did not live too far away, it was easiest for her to come over to Judith and Anthony's large house and for the two of us work together there. Jodie had great technical skills, and she easily did some statistical analyses and constructed a number of tables and figures, which she transferred to my computer. Jodie planned to continue with the analyses, and I would write the first draft of the paper for Jodie and the others to review and comment on.

Early the next morning, Judith drove me to Birmingham Airport and I was on my way back home. My carry-on bag contained special British gifts that Jodie had given me—a beautiful illustrated book called *Tea Time* and a Paddy Bear stuffed animal for a grandchild.

Our study of an all-women team functioning in an extreme environment showed that the team was highly adaptable in dealing with stressful events encountered during the trek; they were flexible in their use of both cognitive and behavioral methods of coping, depending on the situation. A significant theme that emerged was the difference between individual goals and team goals in the daily progress on the trek, that is, pace versus distance. Some wanted to ski as fast as possible each day and break a speed record; others wanted to ski at a slower pace to maintain comfort and safety.

Team members indicated that it was very helpful for team relationships and their daily progress on the ice that the leader listened to their different opinions, even though she made the final decision about the trekking strategies for the next day. However, with two highly dominant individuals in the group, there was occasional tension that had an impact on the team as a whole. Also, consistent with my research on previous expeditions, the importance of honesty in communicating with others, and knowing when to comment on an issue and when not to, was highlighted for both personal and group effectiveness.

The information gained from this study can be applied to understanding some of the team dynamics that might occur during exploration of the Mars surface. There will be considerable autonomy when two astronauts depart from the habitat on a rover and travel some distance from the habitat. It is crucial that these two explorers are in full agreement on their objectives and safety considerations. At this point, a Mars mission is projected to last approximately 2.5 years. Across that time duration, the crew will need to make many operational decisions on their own, both in routine and potential emergency situations. A significant factor in the effectiveness and safety of the crew will be their personal characteristics and attitudes, as well as their formal training. A close assessment of these individual factors as it relates to the mission also is crucial.

22

EPILOGUE

My expedition interests and activities continue. Anders, Jesper and I maintain a close friendship as well as a continued working relationship. We are now collaborating on a small project in Greenland studying two Danish architects who will be living in and testing a lunar habitat they designed. Torben, who got me involved with the Danes and Greenland in the first place, continues to be my source for expert information about Greenland and its Danish military history. I treasure my friendship and contacts with the Danes, and I also am touched that they communicate with me about new personal developments in their lives.

But there are life passages. As Christian, the solo sailor who circumnavigated the globe said when I interviewed him, "I now have Greenland out of my system." Anders is the father of a toddler daughter; instead of sending me photos standing in front of a newly built dogsled, he now sends photos standing in front of a baby carriage with his daughter Ellinore. He also sends occasional photos when he and his girlfriend Lea get together with Christian. More passages: Jodie is the mother of baby girl Shoshana and is on maternity leave.

Both Anders and Jesper returned to the Danish military, Anders on active duty and Jesper with civilian status. Both earned master's degrees from Aalborg University, Anders in organizational psychology/clinical psychology and Jesper in clinical psychology. They spend much of their professional time treating veterans with PTSD and their families. They currently are writing an English-language chapter on team selection and training for a NATO book publication, and I am pleased to continue our ties by working with them on the editing process. Anders also does mental training with a football team, and Jesper is highly involved on a project on team effectiveness. Both are obviously very good fathers and spend quite a bit of time with their children.

My involvement in expedition research changed the trajectory of my professional life. From my first research projects on, I have had wonderful opportunities to meet new and interesting people from many different countries, and travel to and for short periods of time actually live in places that most other people would not have access to. Expeditions were the entry point for my continued years of involvement with NASA's human performance programs.

I think fondly of the great and unique experiences that I had, particularly at Station Nord, where over the course of two trips there, I began to feel that even though it was a short time, I was part of the place, just another worker. And the total cooperation of the Danish Arctic Command, and Kent and Have in Aalborg, is memorable. Because of my expedition research, I became involved with the American and Russian space programs. And who would have thought that as a psychologist I would develop some knowledge about thermal physiology and the inner workings of space suits, because of my Russian connections?

Over the years since my first expedition study in 1986, I have enjoyed talking with every expeditioner that I have met. It gives me a different perspective on life, a great satisfaction in seeing both men and women accomplish sometimes amazing feats of endurance in some of the most inhospitable places on Earth.

On my Arctic trips, I have felt the awesomeness and beauty of nature, and also its strength. There are always lessons learned: there are certain things you can control and other things you cannot, and it is important to know the difference. I hope the nature gods will be kind and allow me to return to one of these truly magnificent places and experience once again the joys of research in spectacular settings. I remember my Russian motto: *zhizn bolshoi priklyucheniye!*—Life is a big adventure!—and this will keep me young, not too bad an outcome.

GREECE DISASTER CONNECTIONS

I have maintained a research track studying stress and coping in a range of extreme environments and situations since the early days of my academic career. Collaboration with my Russian colleague and friend Vadim Kostin on Chernobyl and other disaster-related professional activities was facilitated when he received an academic position at the University of Minnesota in 1992. He and his Moscow colleagues had been actively involved in the World Association of Disaster Medicine (WADEM) for a number of years, presenting papers on their public health-related disaster activities at the WADEM biannual congresses.

I joined WADEM in 1993, and Vadim and I worked together to organize conference sessions focused on the mid- and long-term physical and psychological aftermath of disasters. This topic was of considerable interest for members of the organization because disaster efforts at that time were focused almost entirely on the immediate response to a disaster. My involvement with WADEM was a wonderful opportunity to meet an international group of disaster medicine and public health professionals, and I have maintained many of these professional and personal contacts through the years, particularly with the group at the Athens National School of Public Health.

At the WADEM 1994 congress, friends and colleagues told me they were beginning to appreciate the importance of the psychosocial aftermath of disasters and asked whether I would be willing to form a psychosocial task force as part of the organization. I was very pleased by this request, and along with serving as a board member of the organization, I served as chair and later co-chair of the WADEM psychosocial task force I organized for 10 years, and psychosocial section editor for *Prehospital and Disaster Medicine*, WADEM's official journal.

My professional activities in Greece evolved from conversations with Professor Jeffery Levett at WADEM conferences about psychosocial issues. Jeff is a long-standing member of WADEM and also the founder and first dean of the National School of Public Health (NSPH) in Athens. A considerable focus of his public health efforts has been on populations affected by disasters, a highly relevant issue for Greece because of the many wildfires and earthquakes that strike the region. He was very interested in providing information and training in current psychosocial interventions following a disaster to psychosocial professionals working in Athens and around the country. He also was very keen to sponsor broader conferences and workshops to bring together disaster medicine professionals from countries in the region—the Balkans, Egypt and Turkey.

Figure 6. Year 2000 Sverdrup Centennial Expedition group in front of their boat in Hourglass Bay, Ellesmere Island, Canada.

Source: Photo courtesy of Graeme Magor.

Figure 7. Lars and Guldborg inside the boat with a celebratory Norwegian *kransekake* Liv Dahl baked and brought with for our first evening together.

Source: Photo courtesy of Guldborg Søvik and Lars Hole.

Figure 8. Liv and I departing the Sverdrup expedition Northanger boat site for Grise Fiord via snow machine and komatik (sled).

Source: Photo courtesy of Guldborg Søvik and Lars Hole.

Figure 9. My colleague and scribe Birgit Fink setting up for the interviews with the Sirius Patrol team members at the Danish military Daneborg Station in Greenland, 2012.

Source: Photo courtesy of Gloria Leon.

Figure 10. Relaxing on the "retired" Brave Heart dogsled at Daneborg Station. Sirihus, the main headquarters building, is directly behind me.

Source: Photo courtesy of Gloria Leon.

Figure 11. Birgit and pal in the dog yard at Daneborg Station.
Source: Photo courtesy of Gloria Leon.

Figure 12. Flare directed to Daneborg Station to signal a dogsled patrol team returning from the autumn journey.
Source: Photo courtesy of Anders Kjærgaard.

Figure 13. Long-time colleague Anders Kjærgaard arriving at Qaanaaq/Thule, Greenland, at the end of an extended Sirius Patrol expedition, 2016.

Source: Photo courtesy of Morten Hilmer.

Figure 14. View of Danish military Station Nord, Greenland, outbuildings, site of second Greenland study.

Source: Photo courtesy of Gloria Leon.

Figure 15. Collaborator Jesper Corneliussen mentoring the Station Nord research participants as they practice a computerized cognitive assessment task during a 2014 organizing trip to the station.

Source: Photo courtesy of Gloria Leon.

Figure 16. Communications equipment at Station Nord left over from the Cold War era.

Source: Photo courtesy of Gloria Leon.

Figure 17. Traditional Saturday evening party at Station Nord with a mix of international station and summer workers. The photo was taken the day after I had finished conducting the interviews on the study participants.

Source: Photo courtesy of Gloria Leon.

Figure 18. Station Nord 2016 deployed work group at dinner.
Source: Photo courtesy of Gloria Leon.

Figure 19. The Ice Maidens, an all-military British women's Antarctic expedition team; photo from Antarctica at the finish of their successful traverse of the continent.
Source: Photo courtesy of Natalie Taylor.

Figure 20. British military colleague Jodie Blackadder-Weinstein at Sandhurst in the main building where I conducted the interviews with the expedition team members.

Source: Photo courtesy of Gloria Leon.

GREECE CONNECTIONS

23

ATHENS, PELOPONNESE PENINSULA

2007

Jeff invited me to participate in a public health conference he was organizing in Athens that was held in December 2007 at the President Hotel, close to the NSPH. WADEM was one of the sponsors of this and all of the subsequent Athens workshops, and I attended as the official representative from WADEM. Psychologists from the Ministry of Health and Social Resources and several regional participants attended the conference, including disaster professionals from Serbia and Turkey. I did a presentation on current psychosocial treatment interventions and another on the Utstein Template, WADEM's *Health Disaster Management Guidelines for Evaluation and Research*. Nila Kapor-Stanulovic, a psychology professor from Novi-Sad University in Serbia, was one of the participants whom I met for the first time at the conference. Her presentation focused on her work with UNICEF organizing child- and family-support programs as soon as possible after a disaster or in conflict areas.

Nila and I developed a strong friendship; we bonded in Athens when I accompanied her on an "excursion" to a small shop near NSPH that sold the gourmet Leonidas Belgian chocolates, which she wanted to bring home for her family. We met at other conferences over the next few years, and we always made sure we had some time together. In addition to university academic responsibilities, she was an operational disaster specialist. She has flown on UNICEF planes to many parts of the world to organize psychosocial support. Earlier that year, she was in Beirut for a period of time to design and implement support programs for Palestinian refugee children. Of course, these disaster-related activities take a human toll, and Nila, like many others I have met who do operational work, is very subdued, almost dysphoric, having seen so much suffering.

Professor Leonid Roshal is another example. He is an internationally famous child surgeon and the director of the Moscow Institute of

Emergency Children's Surgery and Traumatology. He is known for his surgical expertise with children who have been gravely wounded; he and his team of surgeons have flown to Chechnya and many international sites immediately following a disaster or terrorist attack. He was the first physician to enter the Moscow theater during the 2002 hostage crisis in which over 170 people were killed, and he also interceded in a hostage crisis situation in Chechnya. Leonid was nominated for the Nobel Peace Prize for these many efforts.

In 2007, I chaired a symposium at the biannual WADEM congress, and Leonid was one of the panel speakers. After his presentation showing before and after slides to explain the surgical procedures he and his support team had performed on terribly wounded children, attendees in the audience had numerous questions for him. I could see that he was getting more and more upset, so after a period of time I called an end to the questions. Leonid and I chatted for a bit after the audience left, and he was in tears. I left him in the room to deal with his feelings and compose himself. How many images of horribly wounded children you have operated on can you stand?

Jeff asked me to stay on following the Athens conference to explore ideas about a future disaster psychology workshop. The group from Turkey also remained to meet with Jeff, Basiliki "Vicky" Papanikolaou, an NSPH faculty member, and others at NSPH to work out some issues related to the emergency and disaster medicine text the Greek and Turkish groups were cowriting. Jeff told me that after their meeting that morning, there was a great deal of controversy about the order of authorship of the book. Jeff had written most of the text, but the Turks were insisting that their organization be listed as first author. There also had been another unrelated problem the previous day; the Turkish delegation threatened to leave, but Vicky assumed the role of diplomat and had resolved that issue. Jeff asked me to chair a meeting that afternoon between the two groups to try to work out the dispute about the book. Oh my!!!

I bravely agreed to do this. When I walked into the room that afternoon there were two groups sitting on either side of a long table glaring at each other. I summoned all of my social skills from my many years of experience chairing university clinical program meetings that sometimes got contentious. There was a Greek translator sitting on my left and a Turkish translator sitting on my right. I started off the meeting by smiling and making some ridiculous comment like "Isn't this so nice. Here we all are, friends and colleagues ready to work together to move the book from the writing stages to a formal text." I'm not sure how this got translated among the different languages, but that was how I started off.

The two sides started talking to each other, but the Turks were adamant that their organization should come first in the line of authorship. There was more back-and-forth discussion, but nothing was resolved at this meeting. Over the next weeks or months, the NSPH group decided that the priority was to have the material published; they eventually agreed to let the Turkish Ministry group take most of the credit. This probably was quite difficult for Jeff and the others; Jeff still referred to Istanbul by its Greek name, Constantinople. When the book finally was published, it was entitled *Health Disaster Management: Hellenic and Turkish Solidarity Building*, in cooperation with WADEM.

After the conference, Elisabeth Petsetakis, an NSPH faculty member, took me on a tour of areas on the Peloponnese peninsula that had been devastated by the wildfires that occurred earlier that year. Greece suffers from severe wildfires almost every summer, but the 2007 conflagration was extremely destructive and many lives were lost. An epidemiological study conducted by Vicky, Jeff and others at the NSPH was in progress to assess the physical and mental health status of the affected population. Attitudes about government and social/religious institutional support to rehabilitate the evacuated areas also was of great interest and relevant to public health policy.

I walked over to the NSPH building to meet Elisabeth for the drive to the Peloponnese peninsula. The NSPH building so reflects the Greek's love of mythology. There is, appropriately, a lovely statue of Hygieia, the goddess of good health at the entrance to the building.

Driving through the peninsula, the high hills and mountains that we passed along the way were charred and barren, and we saw many destroyed homes, fields and burned cars. We stopped at Olympia, the site of the early Olympic Games. It was an incredibly awesome feeling to actually see this ancient historic stadium and walk around the surrounding area. There were burned trees on the hills very close to the stadium, but fortunately the stadium and track were at a lower level and were not affected. As impressed as I was to actually be standing at this ancient site, I couldn't resist—I jogged one lap around the track. That was a historic event for me!

Back in Athens, Jeff, Vicky and I spent more time talking about future plans. They were very committed to establishing a regional disaster center that would include Egypt and the Balkans; they also wanted to continue holding psychosocial disaster workshops for professional education. I thought this was an excellent idea, and I readily agreed to help organize and take part in a psychosocial workshop in Athens. Their plan was to invite both Greek and Egyptian disaster mental health professionals to the next workshop. Along with the specific professional education component, the workshop also had the potential to bring together the key disaster professionals in the region.

I met with Vicky and her assistant Angelos Skembris to discuss strategies for the data analyses of the Peloponnese fires research. Angelos would be my direct contact on this collaborative endeavor, and through the wonders of email we were able to work together in a very productive way.

24

ATHENS, DELPHI, GREEK ISLANDS

2010

The next workshop did not happen as soon as I hoped for because of budget constraints, but it did take place in April 2010. The theme was "Psychosocial Consequences of Natural Disasters." I looked forward to returning to Athens and working directly with Jeff and Vicky. And who could turn down an opportunity to visit Greece? I had contacted psychologist James Shultz, the director of the Center for Disaster and Extreme Event Preparedness at the University of Miami School of Medicine, whom I knew from WADEM conferences and invited him to participate in the workshop. He was very enthusiastic about this opportunity and immediately agreed to take part. Jim spends a great deal of his professional time conducting disaster behavioral health training workshops, and he had produced training materials that would be very valuable for the attendees.

Six physicians from Egypt, with specializations in either psychiatry, emergency medicine or disaster management, attended the workshop. Following introductions, I did a presentation on the importance of treating disorders in addition to PTSD in disaster psychosocial intervention programs, and also the need to include a range of vulnerable populations in treatment planning. My talk the next day was on lessons learned through psychosocial disaster research—Chernobyl, 9/11 and the 1988 Armenian earthquake. Jim did several sessions presenting disaster behavioral health treatment approaches in the context of the catastrophic January 2010 earthquake in Haiti; he also had the attendees break down into small groups for role-playing and further discussion.

Jeff discussed his views on the critical role of peace and human security in improving disaster mitigation, including the role of preparedness, public health and strong governance. On the final day of the workshop, members of the Egyptian delegation described mental health services in Egypt and the current status of psychosocial interventions in response to disasters.

There was a significant international collaborative development that took place at the end of the workshop. A Memorandum of Understanding was agreed upon between the Greek and Egyptian participants, as representatives of their agencies, to work together to establish international standards for preparedness in emergency and disaster situations. There also was agreement to hold a followup workshop in 2011 to continue these efforts, as well as the psychosocial training of professionals from Greece and Egypt.

Along with the content of the formal sessions, it is always an added benefit to meet and talk with people from other countries who have common interests. I had some very warm and interesting conversations with Fahmy Baghat, a young Egyptian psychiatrist who did the disaster response presentation; and Jihan K., a professor of anesthesiology and an emergency medicine physician in Cairo. Jihan was formally dressed in a long robe and a keffiyeh, a white head scarf covering. Fahmy told me that his wife also was a physician, and described the differences in their professional lives related to their gender. In separate conversations with Jihan, I also heard about her family life and what her professional life was like.

Some of these conversations with the Egyptians took place after the conference sessions, while we were on a sightseeing tour of the Acropolis. There is an interesting cultural contrast that can be seen on the group photo on the balcony of the Acropolis Museum. At the right end of the line of people, I am standing with Jihan, in a keffiyeh, with my arm around her; at the other end of the line is our Greek young woman student guide, wearing a low-cut blouse.

My Athens hosts arranged for Jim and I to do an excursion to Delphi after the conference was over. Delphi is an ancient and spectacular sight—buildings, amphitheater and stadium high up on the mountain, and a nearby lower area that includes the sacred circular Tholos of Delphi structure. The beauty of the marble statues in the museum took my breath away, as did the steep climb to the top of the mountain to see the stadium. Certainly in Greece, there is no end to the awesome sights—ancient temples, statues, museums and continuing new excavations.

Jim returned to the United States the following day, but the Egyptian group stayed on for an additional day related to their flight arrangements. They were very happy and excited to have the chance to go shopping at the Marks and Spencer department store in central Athens, which promised good quality clothing at fair prices. Back at the hotel following their shopping adventure, one of the men enlisted Fahmy for some help. He had purchased some clothing for his wife, and he wanted to make sure it was the right size. He thought his wife was about Fahmy's height, so with much ado and lots of laughter Fahmy stood in as the model. Jihan very happily took me to a private room and showed me the clothes she had bought. It was a different experience to see that she wore jeans under her robe!

That evening, Jihan stayed at the hotel, but Fahmy, another of the Egyptian group and I went on a Metro excursion. My two companions already were experts on the Metro system, and the original plan was to take the Metro to the port of Piraeus for dinner; however, part of the Metro system that would get us to the port area was closed. Instead, we went to the Plaka, the old city adjacent to the Acropolis; we walked around for awhile and then found a restaurant for dinner. We had a really great evening, dining at a restaurant with a spectacular view of the Acropolis.

There is nothing like sitting at an outdoor restaurant and looking up at the Acropolis, perched high on a cliff overlooking the city and lit up at night. In all of my trips to Athens, I never tired of the experience. And to top it off, the Ministry treated me to a full-day boat excursion the next day, the boat stopping at three quite different Greek islands. And I swam in the Aegean Sea!

Earlier on this visit, Jeff and his daughter Mirella took Jim and me to a small café in the center of the city. We were the only ones in the place speaking English, and it was a nice feeling to be with local people. The food was very special, including sea urchins and other kinds of seafood that one would not encounter in more tourist-oriented restaurants. It was an adventure with a pleasant end—the food was delicious, although sometimes it was better not to know what you were eating!

25

ATHENS, CORINTH, ISTANBUL, CAPPADOCIA

2011

Jeff and Vicky put in a great deal of effort to obtain support from the Ministry of Health and Social Resources for a follow-up workshop. Their efforts were successful and the *International Workshop: Greece and Egypt* was held in October 2011 at the President Hotel. For this workshop, I wanted to invite a psychologist with a somewhat different treatment orientation, to supplement the workshop training the attendees had received the previous year. I asked Professor James Halpern to be the key psychology presenter at the workshop. James founded and was the current director of the academic Institute for Disaster Mental Health at SUNY New Paltz. In addition to his university courses, he and his colleagues organized training seminars for personnel at local and state government agencies. He also had direct experience providing psychosocial treatment to disaster victims. After 9/11, he was the leader of the first team of mental health workers at Ground Zero. I was very pleased that he immediately agreed to participate.

Greece is always a beautiful place to visit, and it is easy to forget the Athens traffic while awestruck at all of the ancient history and beautiful surroundings. I arrived in Athens two days before the workshop, to deal with jet lag and also take a day trip to Corinth to see the Temple ruins and the ancient fortress housing the archaeological museum. The second day, I just wandered around the Athens Plaka and walked up the steep path to the Acropolis. By this time, I had a favorite restaurant in the Plaka—Dionysos, with an outdoor courtyard and a view of the Acropolis.

Jeff and Vicky's efforts to organize this workshop involved a great deal of collaboration with Professor Mohsen Gadallah, who was the chair of the Department of Community Medicine in the Faculty of Medicine at Ain Shams University in Cairo. This was an extremely challenging period for the Egyptians. The Arab Spring demonstrations in Cairo had begun in April 2011; numerous casualties were treated at their hospital, and there was a change of government. One of the Egyptian participants was extremely distressed; he told me that he and his neighbors were taking turns guarding their houses every night to prevent break-ins and looting.

The workshop began in a very formal way with introductions by a number of Ministry officials, Jeff, Anastasia Roumelioti, NSPH Dean, Dimitry Pyrros, former WADEM president and head of the ambulance services in Athens, and Mohsen Gadallah. I did one several-hour presentation, but James had the burden (James fortified himself early each morning with a walk to a nearby Starbucks for a high test coffee). James's training activities extended over 1.5 days; the theme was *Core Psychosocial Practices in Complex Emergencies*, including material on self-care for disaster and trauma workers.

Following the Memorandum of Understanding signed the previous year, another emphasis of the conference was on how to formalize a disaster response working relationship between Greece and Egypt, in part under the WADEM umbrella. All parties were eager to form collaborating disaster centers in their countries. Mohsen suggested that the focus of the center in Cairo should be on psychosocial factors, which he termed a "center of competence." He and others felt strongly that workshops could provide substantive training in how to integrate psychosocial interventions into emergency medical services during disasters, particularly mass casualty incidents.

In order to move this concept along, there was agreement among the discussants to repeat the current workshop in Cairo the following year, with a large group of Egyptian specialists and a smaller group from Greece. I was asked to lead the workshop in collaboration with James Halpern, with both of us serving as representatives from WADEM. James and I were in firm agreement with this understanding of the importance of psychosocial support among emergency medicine specialists and that we would be involved in these future activities.

Mohsen and his colleagues also asked me whether I would be interested in organizing a research project on the psychological effects of physical trauma suffered during the Arab Spring demonstrations. He proposed that the subjects chosen for the study would be patients treated at their Cairo hospital who were injured during the demonstrations; the comparison group would be patients who were admitted to the same hospital emergency room whose physical injuries were caused by other events. This topic was highly relevant for disaster mental health and the focus of the center they wished to create in Cairo. I agreed to take the lead in developing the research protocol. The plan was that Vicky, working with Mohsen, would take primary responsibility for conducting the study.

We finished the workshop and discussions about future directions with great hopes of continuing these contacts through the workshop planned for the following year in Cairo. In addition, Jeff hoped that eventually disaster professionals from the Balkans would be included in planning for a regional disaster center. I consulted with Vicky on a protocol for the Cairo study; we selected a measure of psychological distress and also a questionnaire assessing attitudes about the control a person feels over the events that happen to them.

That evening, Jeff took James and me to an Armenian restaurant in the old city. We were seated on the second floor of this restaurant, enjoying impressive views of the lighted Acropolis. James kept commenting on the beauty and tranquility of the experience, and I certainly had this feeling as well. Later in the evening, there was live music and song at the restaurant, and we all had an excellent time. These special experiences in Athens always were a great finale to an interesting and stimulating workshop.

Jeff and his family were wonderful hosts, and I got to know the family quite well. Jeff and his daughter Mirella usually came over to the hotel the evening that I arrived, and we would sit together on the hotel rooftop terrace and catch up on our personal and professional lives. Jeff's wife Tina was an excellent cook, and visits to their apartment also allowed me to enjoy the fantastic view of Mount Lycabettus from their apartment windows. Jeff's other daughter Mellissa and her son Jeffakos lived with them, and it was a pleasure to see him grow and speak English on my visits, which for a period of time were happening every year.

After the conference, James took advantage of being in Greece and flew to Santorini for a few days to relax and work on a manuscript. I usually try to include a side trip at the end of professional meetings and I flew to Istanbul and spent four nights there.

Istanbul has its own glorious ambience—the Blue Mosque, Hagia Sophia Museum, Basilica Cistern, open market places, many historic sights and its location at the end of the Bosporus Canal. I booked a room at the Hotel Poem, a small hotel with even tinier rooms in the Asian part of the city, very close to all of the major attractions. True to its name, each room had a poem on the hallway door! On several days in the city, I worked a few hours on my laptop each morning sitting in the hotel courtyard and then went sightseeing. The evening view of the lighted Blue Mosque that I enjoyed while sitting in a restaurant brought the same feelings of awe and tranquility as my experiences looking at the Acropolis at night.

I arranged prior to the trip to have a guided tour of Jewish Istanbul. There have been Jewish communities in what is now Turkey for over 2,500 years; the greatest influx came when Jews were welcomed to Turkey after they were expelled from Spain in 1492. However, at present the situation was quite different. Because of synagogue bombings and other terrorist attacks against the Jewish community, security was very tight and I had to send passport information and other documents before the tour could be confirmed. A large historic synagogue is now a museum, showing the history of the area that extended back to ancient times. It was a very interesting visit, observing and reading the displays showing that there were settled communities and Jewish merchants who moved back and forth through the area for thousands of years.

One day, I took a boat excursion that went all the way to the Black Sea. This was quite an exciting experience; the Black Sea takes on an almost mystical feeling for me. It borders on so many countries of the former Soviet Union. After World War II, my father's two surviving brothers, their families and sister lived in Odessa on the Black Sea. I kept saying to myself with wonder, "This is it. This is the Black Sea."

Another day, I flew to Cappadocia on a day tour. This is an amazing place, full of hoodoo formations of many shapes and sizes. There is an underground city that was used by the early Christians as a refuge; the tour I was on took us through several rooms that had been carved out of the rock. Hot air balloons also are a feature of the area, but I didn't have enough time to squeeze that in. I was probably fortunate—a man on my tour was totally shook up. He had been on a balloon flight earlier that day; the balloon had caught fire and they almost crashed into the mountain wall. He said they barely escaped with their lives. So it did seem fitting at the end of the tour to buy a traditional evil eye, which I purchased on a keychain.

I noticed in Istanbul many signs for tours to Gallipoli. I asked an Australian WADEM colleague about this some time later; he indicated that Gallipoli is a sacred place for Australians and New Zealanders, and also for people from Turkey. There were so many lives lost there during World War I, and both adversaries revere the place.

Then it was time to start my trip back home. I took a late evening flight from Istanbul back to Athens that got in after midnight. It was too late an arrival to deal with hotels, and I simply hung out at the airport until my early morning flight. I noticed that I wasn't the only one doing this.

26

INTERLUDE

Unfortunately, the following year was an extremely difficult period for both Greece and Egypt. While all parties were willing and ready to work together for a 2012 workshop in Egypt, political events, economic difficulties in Egypt and the extremely severe and worsening austerity in Greece made it impossible to hold a workshop in Cairo.

The austerity measures imposed by the European Union on Greece had a devastating effect on all academic institutions, and the National School of Public Health was in dire financial straits. Jeff and Vicky were trying very hard to obtain funds from the Ministry to conduct a mental health survey of the population. They hoped that these data would provide greater financial support to the population in need and in the process maintain the activities of the School.

Jeff asked whether I would return and do a small workshop for the Ministry of Health and Social Resources psychologists and social workers, and meet with some city officials. He also asked for my collaboration in developing the research protocol for the mental health survey; he felt my input would be helpful in obtaining funds for the project from the head of the Ministry. At this point, the 2007 Wildfires study had already been published. In addition, the research with our Egyptian colleagues was underway.

The Greek Wildfires study documented the extreme psychological distress in the group affected by the fires compared to the non-affected control group. However, both groups rated unemployment and poverty as the most significant problem in their region. The highest proportion of ratings in both groups indicated that the Church was the most trusted institution; the Government was the least trusted. These findings clearly pointed to the public health needs of the overall population and the relationship between overall poor quality of life and the extremely difficult economic situation in the country.

The research and data analysis of the Cairo Arab Spring study were completed prior to my next trip to Greece. The findings from this study showed that the group injured in the Cairo epicenter during the violent demonstrations experienced greater psychological distress than the group with physical trauma from other causes. The perception of locus of control was significantly associated with psychological distress; participants in both groups who felt that the events that happened in their lives were outside of their personal control (external control orientation) scored higher on the measure of psychological distress than participants with an internal control orientation. These findings suggest a relationship between perceived helplessness in controlling one's life circumstances and psychological distress.

27

ATHENS, KEPHALONIA

2012

Once again, I traveled to Athens in October 2012 and was housed at the President Hotel (the woman supervisor of the dining room knew me at this point because all of the workshops were held at the hotel. I was happy that my handy kiosk outside of the hotel where I bought Cola Light was still there). During the last several years, there were numerous strikes in Athens and other Greek cities. The hotel helpfully always put up notices in the elevators listing the dates and times that different groups would be on strike. On one of my visits, both the air traffic controllers and the taxi and bus drivers were on strike the same day. Truly a reflection of the major economic difficulties faced at all levels of Greek society.

Jeff and his daughter Mirella met me at the hotel on the evening of my arrival, and it felt like a family homecoming to see them again and have a drink and some snacks on the rooftop lounge looking out over the city. I spent the next day dealing with jet lag and working on some of my materials.

The following morning, Angelos, whom I continued to work closely with on the Greek fires study, assumed his role as escort. But this time, our first activity was taking a bus and then a taxi to a specific bank. Angelos had a check in my name for my expenses, but the check could only be cashed at this particular bank. The NSPH people I would be working with were not allowed to be reimbursed for their own expenses, so the solution was to add on to my expenses, and then I paid for everything. It was a reasonable arrangement. We had to wait a long time at the bank for the correct teller, and then I was handed a thick envelope with brand new 100 Euro bills. It felt just like the Mafia! From the bank, we went directly to a building of the Ministry of Health and Social Resources where the psychosocial group had their offices, to get ready for my presentation.

Greetings with Theodore Mousterakis, head of the Social Intervention Department of the Ministry, and his staff also felt a bit like a homecoming, and there were some friendly hugs all around. My presentation focused on different methods of providing psychosocial support at different phases of a disaster to promote community resilience. I also presented information on European Union (EU) and WADEM recommendations for psychosocial care plans at national, regional and local levels.

Following my talk, the attendees were quite open in expressing their concerns about current public health problems. They shared their extreme frustration about the poor services available for the people in need in the country and their lack of power to obtain funds to help those who so badly needed basic resources. We also talked about the survey Jeff and Vicky were trying to initiate, to provide documentation of the local area's health status and quality of life.

Following the meeting, Jeff, Vicky, Angelos and I drove to the city center for a meeting with Kalliopi Giannopoulou, Athens Deputy Mayor for Social Policy and Solidarity. (I love those Greek names!) The head social worker for Athens was there as well for the meeting. Mayor Giannopoulou described the extreme needs of the vulnerable populations in Athens, including those with physical and mental health problems. She described the system of food distribution centers and shelters, and indicated that there were approximately 1,400 homeless people in Athens at that time. She strongly supported the idea of a survey of the homeless in Athens in order to improve services for them (Mayor Giannopoulou was an extremely warm and outgoing person. For several years after this visit, I received beautiful Christmas cards from her).

Later in the day, ironically, after Jeff, Vicky, Angelos and I had eaten lunch at a very nice restaurant, we drove to a food distribution center where sometimes seven hundred people a day wait in line for food; this included families, both native Greek and immigrants. The director of the distribution center expressed concern that there would be an even larger number of people seeking help as the economic crisis worsened. This visit was indeed a very sobering experience. There was a long line of single people and entire families with downtrodden faces waiting their turn for a small amount of food. I thought of the director's comments that the situation likely was going to get worse.

The next day, Jeff, Angelos and I went to a meeting at the National Center for Social Solidarity (EKKA). The Center coordinates the provision of social support services to people in crisis situations. Theodore and others from different departments in the Ministry also attended. Theodore talked about the need to improve the cooperation among agencies in responding to a disaster. Jeff brought up the idea of providing disaster mental health training for the EKKA staff and described the different psychosocial training workshops I had organized over the past few years. I spent some time talking about disaster mental health interventions and the timeline for initiating different responses, as relevant to their agency.

I was getting used to eating lunch at three o'clock in the afternoon. After the meeting, we went back to NSPH, and then Jeff, Angelos and I walked over to a small café in the neighborhood. The proprietor knew Jeff, and he filled large plates of whatever he was serving for each of us and produced glasses of wine. We were quite hungry at this point, and I smiled as I watched Jeff and Angelos down this delicious food with great gusto (I was doing the same).

We still had work to do. I met with Jeff, Vicky and Angelos the next day at NSPH. The first priority was to work together on the development of a demographic and physical and mental health survey instrument that would have a more narrow focus on the homeless population of Athens. Also, Jeff and Vicky were very committed to NSPH sponsoring continuing education workshops for psychosocial professionals. We agreed to plan for a psychosocial disaster training workshop for the following year in coordination with the staff at EKKA and to ask James Halpern whether he would take the lead on the workshop presentations.

Angelos and I worked together on the data from the Cairo study comparing groups who suffered physical trauma caused by demonstration violence with groups with physical trauma from other causes. The results of the study showed greater distress in the group that had experienced violence; however, subjects in both groups who felt they had little control over their lives also indicated greater psychological distress.

I had arranged for a side trip to the beautiful Aegean Sea island of Kephalonia to follow my time in Athens. The trip to Kephalonia also ended up as a break from the really depressing situation I just had seen firsthand in Athens, which affected the population at all levels (at this time, both of Jeff's daughters had lost their jobs, and they all were living in the Levett apartment, supported primarily by Jeff's pension).

Kephalonia is in an area of relatively high earthquake activity; the island was struck by a large earthquake several years earlier, but most structures had been rebuilt. I was attracted to Kephalonia by the movie *Captain Corelli's Mandolin*, starring Nicolas Cage and Penelope Cruz, filmed on the island. I had used the internet to contact a tour company in Kephalonia and requested a tour where I could see some of the natural scenery filmed in the movie. The next day, I received a message from someone named

Konstantinos, saying that he was my man, he had been a tour guide and also had served as an extra in the film. You can't get better than that!

I was not disappointed with my tour; the island is totally gorgeous with high mountains, beautiful beaches and the sea, a castle and ancient ruins. A fresh fish lunch while sitting at a café looking out at the Aegean Sea and a private island in the distance was not a bad way to spend a few hours. Konstantinos showed me the different villas where the actors had stayed, the sights from the movie and shared a bit of gossip. However, the film did not accurately show some of the actual landscape; Konstantinos explained that in certain scenes of the film, different backgrounds were spliced together to look like one location.

It was very interesting to talk with Konstantinos and hear about their daily lives. Tourism was the main industry on the island. He told me that with Greece joining the EU, all of the Greek fishermen were required to give up their fishing licenses. This seemed to me a terrible cultural blow; fishing as a livelihood is so much a part of the Greek culture. Also, as with any island location, much of what is needed for life on the island has to be imported, and this is quite expensive. However, since farming is the second-largest industry on the island, the villagers do not have to rely heavily on imported food.

Back again to Athens for an overnight stay and then home. I was hopeful that a survey of the Athens homeless and another workshop would be possible, but given the severe austerity in Greece, I wasn't sure whether there would be funds available.

The economic and political situation in Greece continued to worsen. While plans were made to hold a workshop in 2014, the funds did not come through and the workshop had to be cancelled. Also, the NSPH and Ministry groups were never able to obtain funds for even a small survey of the homeless population in Athens. But thoughts of Greece and my friends there stayed with me.

28

ATHENS, TEMPLE OF POSEIDON, MARATHON

2014

In the spring of 2014, I decided to take a trip to Athens, simply to visit with the Levetts and my other friends. Vicky heard that I was coming; she and her daughter met me at the airport and we drove directly to a restaurant for lunch. Vicky had returned a few days earlier from Cyprus, where she was working with government groups on public health projects. She still had a dream of continuing with the disaster workshops in coordination with the Egyptians, but she acknowledged that it just was not possible at that time because of the economic situation.

I stayed at the President Hotel yet again. The city was in the midst of a garbage strike that had been going on for quite some time, and the sidewalks were filled with large garbage bags. But it was great to see the Levett family and to bring grandson Jeffakos more English books. It also was Jeff's daughter Mirella's birthday, and I was part of the dinner celebration at their apartment. One day, Jeff, his wife Tina, Jeffakos and I drove down the Attica Peninsula to walk among the ruins of the beautiful Temple of Poseidon. Later, we had an early dinner at a seaside restaurant. I always wanted to see the Temple up close; it is very visible on the descending flight into Athens.

On another day during my stay, Jeff, a colleague and I drove along the sea, stopped for coffee and then turned inland to visit a monastery. Our next stop was Marathon, the site of the historic 490 BC Battle of Marathon. According to legend, a Greek soldier ran from Marathon to Athens to announce the defeat of the Persians; the distance was approximately 40 km, close to the distance of modern marathons. There is an impressive statue at Marathon of a Greek soldier who supposedly ran the distance, and I have a few photos of our group taking turns standing in front of the statue.

Later, we feasted on an incredible meal at a beachside restaurant. The owner of the restaurant took us inside and showed us the refrigerator case with the fish that had been caught that day. There were pictures of him on the wall from the time when he had made his living as a fisherman. It was a delightful day, and I treasured the many beautiful sights along the way. It also was relaxing to simply visit without any meetings or presentations.

29

EPILOGUE

I returned home hoping that the public health efforts of the group at NSPH and other institutions, who were so dedicated to their work, would continue. Unfortunately, yet again, they were unable to obtain funds for additional workshops and the survey. However, Jeff continues activities to promote peace in the Balkans; he has organized and been the keynote speaker at a number of conferences in the Balkans, focused on young people as the hope for the future. He recently received a major international honor—the International Gusi Peace Prize, Asia's equivalent of the Nobel Peace Prize, awarded to him at an event in the Philippines.

Vicky is still hoping to organize more psychosocial workshops. And Angelos is consulting with a company in the UK; he devises research projects for the development of sensor-based technologies. The Levett daughters are employed again in professional positions, and Jeffakos is now a teenager! Although time has passed, we all remain strongly committed to holding more training workshops and renewing the regional ties, if that is at all possible.

Following one of the workshops, NSPH Dean Roumelioti presented me with a beautiful marble head of Hygieia, the goddess of good health. It is a lovely replica of the original, located at a temple in Epidauros, Greece. The bust is sitting on a shelf in my office. It is always a great memory of my friends and colleagues in Athens.

Figure 21. Psychosocial disaster workshop sponsored by the Athens National School of Public Health with Greek and Egyptian public health and psychiatry participants, in Athens, Greece, 2010.

Source: Photo courtesy of Gloria Leon.

Figure 22. Psychosocial disaster workshop group gathered around Professor Jeffrey Levett (center), founder and first dean, Athens National School of Public Health, prior to departure for the official banquet.

Source: Photo courtesy of Gloria Leon.

AFTERWORD

Life continues to be a series of passages. After serving on NASA Human Research Program (HRP) panels for many years, I decided that the February 2020 Human Factors and Behavioral Performance peer review panel I chaired would be my last. It was getting more tiring to travel to Washington each time, and the organizers really needed to get younger people involved. I was pleasantly surprised and really touched when Tom Williams, the head of the HRP Human Factors and Behavioral Performance element, presented me with a newly designed space poster and an HRP patch. The patch had actually been in space; it was sent up in a SpaceX Dragon spacecraft that was docked to the International Space Station for 21 days. What a fantastic momento!

But my contacts and collaboration with NASA have not ended, just the focus from serving in advisory capacities. I will be working with several in the HRP group on a research project for the upcoming SIRIUS-2020 Mars analog mission; a mixed-gender crew of three Americans and three Russians who will live and work together for eight months in the Mars simulation chamber in Moscow. Our individual study will examine relationships between personality factors and team effectiveness, with a particular emphasis on the process of conflict resolution.

I am delighted to continue collaborating with my Danish friends on expedition studies. Working together also keeps me involved in their passages through life, and I am always glad to help out with any tasks related to their professional activities. Through Zoom calls, it is very easy to stay in touch. I said "hi" in English to my friend Anders's toddler Ellinor a few weeks ago—the first time I saw her "in person."

Together with Anders and others, we currently are organizing materials for another project in Greenland, this time involving two young Danish architects who for three months will be living in and testing a lunar habitat they designed and built. This study is particularly timely—it maps with NASA's planned 2024 Artemis mission to land two astronauts on the surface of the moon, where they will live in a habitat and carry out some surface exploration. So, more evaluations of stress and coping in extreme environments, in this case with an actual application for a near-future space mission.

I have been officially retired from the University of Minnesota since 2006, but I still have my office at the University and the support of the department chair and faculty to continue my professional activities. While I have been thinking about writing a memoir about my professional experiences for some time, the stimulus for actually doing so was the stay-at-home lockdown restrictions because of the COVID-19 pandemic. These past several months at home have provided a major chunk of time to write relatively undisturbed, although not for good reasons.

As I write, the world continues to be in the midst of a pandemic with no real end in sight, and there is major turmoil in numerous countries in response to human rights abuses and police brutality. At the present time the world does not seem to be a very friendly place. I have looked back on my life and professional career, as many others do in difficult circumstances, and tried to focus on the positive as much as possible.

One of the greatest differences I see over time is the change in the acceptance of women in professional roles. My sex discrimination suit against Rutgers was filed 47 years ago; some of the situations that women experienced at that time could not happen so easily and maliciously right now. That is not to say that we live in a perfect world, but there is no question that the professional landscape is better now in terms of the affirmation of the abilities of women and their rightful presence in the workplace, and that it is possible to combine family and a career.

When I think about the times I spent in the Soviet Union/Russia and the people I met, it is a remembrance of history as well as specific individuals. I was traveling back and forth over a five-year time period when an entire country disappeared. Because of my research activities and interests, the people I met and worked with at the various institutes were at the highest levels of their profession. They were coping with life within an authoritarian regime that suddenly changed quite dramatically.

The opportunity to travel to Chernobyl, only six years after this devastating disaster, taught me as nothing else could about the frailty of human life and the environment. But so many of my memories of that period just make me smile. What adventures I had with my Russian friends! In our travels, we dealt with whatever came our way with humor and laughter. I could relate to the Russian *dusha* (soul), the drama and the coping and resilience dealing with their daily lives.

My disaster-related activities with the National School of Public Health group in Athens, organizing psychosocial conferences and helping with research, also was very interesting and productive. As with the earlier work with the Russians, my involvement expanded over a period of time to sometimes annual trips. It was a good feeling to contribute to the professional expertise of local psychologists by holding disaster training workshops. Just as important on a personal level, I established good and lasting friendships through these professional activities. And what a wonderful opportunity to experience the incredible beauty and history of Greece.

Another happening I think about is how fortunate I have been to be able to combine my scholarly work with my love of adventure and nature. The experiences that I had, spending time in places most people never would have been able to go to, was interesting and so much fun. I also had the opportunity to write up the research studies related to these experiences, have the material published in scientific journals and then get recognition for it, like being invited to collaborate with NASA or the British Royal Air Force. This combination of science and adventure was the ultimate treat.

So, this is an Afterword, not an obituary. I hope to continue to be active professionally but yet have time to "smell the roses." I look forward to more projects and adventures. And I still try to follow my same signature motto by saying, once again, *Zhizn bolshoi priklyucheniye!* (Life is a big adventure!)

SELECTED REFERENCES

Academia

Leon, Gloria R., and Karen Chamberlain. 1973. "Comparison of Daily Eating Habits and Emotional States of Overweight Persons Successful or Unsuccessful In Maintaining a Weight Loss." *Journal of Consulting and Clinical Psychology* 41, no. 1: 108–15.

———. 1973. "Emotional Arousal, Eating Patterns and Body Image as Differential Factors Associated with Varying Success in Maintaining a Weight Loss." *Journal of Consulting and Clinical Psychology* 40, no. 3: 474–80.

Leon, Gloria R. 1974. *Case Histories of Deviant Behavior: A Social Learning Analysis.* Boston: Holbrook Press.

———. 1974. "Personality Change in the Specially Admitted Disadvantaged Student after One Year in College." *Journal of Clinical Psychology* 30, no. 4: 522–28.

———. 1975. "Personality, Body Image and Eating Pattern Changes in Overweight Persons after Weight Loss." *Journal of Clinical Psychology* 31, no. 4: 618–23.

———, James N. Butcher, Max Kleinman, Alan Goldberg, and Moshe Almagor. 1981. "Survivors of the Holocaust and Their Children: Current Status and Adjustment." *Journal of Personality and Social Psychology* 41, no. 3: 503–16.

———, Andrew R. Lucas, Robert C. Colligan, Richard J. Ferdinande, and John Kamp. 1985. "Body Image, Sexual Attitudes, and Family Interaction Patterns in Anorexia Nervosa." *Journal of Abnormal Child Psychology* 13, no. 2: 245–58.

———, Kathleen Carroll, Benita Chernyk, and Stephen Finn. 1985. "Binge Eating and Associated Habit Patterns within College Student and Identified Bulimic Populations." *International Journal of Eating Disorders* 4, no. 1: 43–57.

———, Stephen Hjemboe, and Yossef Ben-Porath. 1990. "Coping Patterns and Current Functioning in a Group of Vietnam and Vietnam-Era Nurses." *Journal of Social and Clinical Psychology* 9, no. 3: 334–53.

———, Jayne A. Fulkerson, Cheryl L. Perry, and Robert Cudeck. 1993. "Personality and Behavioral Vulnerabilities Associated with Risk Status for Eating Disorders in Adolescent Girls." *Journal of Abnormal Psychology* 102, no. 3: 438–44.

———, Jayne A. Fulkerson, Cheryl L. Perry, and Mary Early-Zald. 1995. "Prospective Analysis of Personality and Behavioral Vulnerabilities and Gender Influences in the Later Development of Disordered Eating." *Journal of Abnormal Psychology* 104, no. 1: 140–49.

The Russian Drama

Koscheyev, Victor S., Vladimir K. Martens, Alexander A. Kosenkov, Michael A. Lartsev, and Gloria R. Leon. 1993. "Psychological Functioning of Chernobyl Nuclear Power Plant Operators after the Nuclear Disaster." *Journal of Traumatic Stress* 6, no. 4: 561–68.

———, Gloria R. Leon, Andrej V. Gourine, and Valerie N. Gourine. 1997. "The Psychosocial Aftermath of the Chernobyl Disaster in an Area of Relatively Low Contamination." *Prehospital and Disaster Medicine* 12, no. 1: 41–46.

Leon, Gloria R., Jayne A. Fulkerson, Ian R. Luepker, and Yuri Yunov. 1997. "Perceptions of Group and Personal Influences and Effectiveness among Disabled and Able-Bodied Members of a Russian Wheelchair Expedition." *International Journal of Sport Psychology* 28, no. 2: 172–84.

Expedition Adventures

Leon, Gloria R., Carl McNally, and Yossef S. Ben-Porath. 1989. "Personality Characteristics, Mood, and Coping Patterns in a Successful North Pole Expedition Team." *Journal of Research in Personality* 23, no. 2: 162–79.

Leon, Gloria R. 1991. "Individual and Group Process Characteristics of Polar Expedition Teams." *Environment and Behavior* 23, no. 6: 723–48.

———, Ruth Kanfer, Richard G. Hoffman, and Lonnie Dupre. 1991. "Interrelationships of Personality and Coping in a Challenging Extreme Situation." *Journal of Research in Personality* 25, no. 4: 357–71.

Kahn, Pauline M., and Gloria R. Leon. 1994. "Group Climate and Individual Functioning in an All-Women Antarctic Expedition Team." *Environment and Behavior* 26, no. 5: 669–97.

Leon, Gloria R., Ruth Kanfer, Richard G. Hoffman, and Lonnie Dupre. 1994. "Group Processes and Task Effectiveness in a Soviet-American Expedition Team." *Environment and Behavior* 26, no. 2: 149–65.

Leon, Gloria R., and Victor S. Koscheyev. 1996. "Applications of U.S.-Russian Expedition Research To Aerospace Settings." In *Proceedings of the 26th International Conference on Environmental Systems*, SAE Technical Paper Series 961612. Warrendale, PA: SAE International.

———. 1996. "Expedition Applications to Long Duration Space Missions." In *Space V. Proceedings of the Fifth International Conference on Space '96* Vol. 2, edited by Stewart W. Johnson, 997–1001. New York: American Society of Civil Engineers.

Leon, Gloria R. 2002. "Conscientiousness and Work Performance while Suffering from Acute Mountain Sickness: A Case Report." *Aviation, Space and Environmental Medicine* 73, no. 4: 388–91.

———, Mera M. Atlis, Deniz Ones, and Graeme Magor. 2002. "A One-Year Three Couple Expedition as a Crew Analog for a Mars Mission." *Environment and Behavior* 34, no. 5: 672–700.

———, and Gro M. Sandal. 2003. "Women and Couples in Isolated, Extreme Environments: Applications for Long-Duration Missions." *Acta Astronautica* 53, no. 4: 259–67.

Atlis, Mera M., Gloria R. Leon, Gro M. Sandal, and Michael Infante. 2004. "Decision Processes and Interactions during a Two Woman Traverse of Antarctica." *Environment and Behavior* 36, no. 3: 402–23.

Leon, Gloria R. 2005. "Men and Women in Space." *Aviation, Space, and Environmental Medicine* 76, no. 6, Suppl: B84–B88.

Sandal, Gro M., Gloria R. Leon, and Lawrence A. Palinkas. 2006. "Human Challenges in Polar and Space Environments." *Reviews in Environmental Science and Bio/Technology* 5, no. 2: 281–96.

Leon, Gloria R., and Andrea Scheib. 2007. "Personality Influences on a Two-Man Arctic Expedition, Impact on Spouse, and the Return Home." *Aviation, Space and Environmental Medicine* 78, no. 5: 526–29.

———, Gro M. Sandal, and Eric Larsen. 2011. "Human Performance In Polar Environments." *Journal of Environmental Psychology* 31, no. 4: 353–60.

———, Gro M. Sandal, Birgit Fink, and Paul Ciofani. 2011. "Positive Experiences and Personal Growth in a Two-Man North Pole Expedition Team." *Environment and Behavior* 43, no. 5: 710–31.

Kjærgaard, Anders, Gloria R. Leon, Noah C. Venables, and Birgit A. Fink. 2013. "Personality, Personal Values and Growth in Military Special Unit Patrol Teams Operating in a Polar Environment." *Military Psychology* 25, no. 1: 13–22.

———, Gloria R. Leon, and Birgit A. Fink. 2015. "Personal Challenges, Communication Processes, and Team Effectiveness in Military Special Patrol Teams Operating in a Polar Environment." *Environment and Behavior* 47, no. 6: 644–66.

Kjærgaard, Anders, Gloria R. Leon, and Noah C. Venables. 2015. "The Psychological Process of Reintegration following a Nine Month/260 Day Solo Sailboat Circumnavigation of the Globe." *Scandinavian Journal of Psychology* 56, no. 2: 198–202.

———. 2015. "The 'Right Stuff' for a Solo Sailboat Circumnavigation of the Globe." *Environment and Behavior* 4, no. 10: 1147–71.

Leon, Gloria R., and Noah C. Venables. 2015. "Fearless Temperament and Overconfidence in an Unsuccessful Special Forces Polar Expedition." *Aerospace Medicine and Human Performance* 86, no. 5: 567–70.

Corneliussen, Jesper G., Gloria R. Leon, Anders Kjærgaard, Birgit A. Fink, and Noah C. Venables. 2017. "Individual Traits, Personal Values, Conflict Resolution in an Isolated, Confined, Extreme Environment." *Aerospace Medicine and Human Performance* 88, no. 6: 535–43.

Blackadder-Weinstein, Jodie, Gloria R. Leon, Rachel C. Norris, Noah C. Venables, and Michael Smith. 2019. "Individual Attributes, Values, and Goals of an All-Military Women Antarctic Expedition." *Aerospace Medicine and Human Performance* 90, no. 1: 18–25.

Greece Disaster Connections

Sundnes, Knut O., Marvin L., Birnbaum, and Elaine D. Birnbaum. 2003. "Health Disaster Management Guidelines for Evaluation and Research in the Utstein Style." *Prehospital and Disaster Medicine* 17, no. 3: 1–168.

Papanikolaou, Vasiliki, Gloria R. Leon, John Kyriopoulos, Jeffrey Levett, and Eleftherios Pallis. 2011. "Surveying the Ashes: The Experience from the 2007

Peloponnese Wildfires Six Months after the Disaster." *Prehospital and Disaster Medicine* 26, no. 2: 79–89.

———, Mohsen Gadallah, Gloria R. Leon, Efthalia Massou, Gerasimos Prodromitis, Angelos Skembris, and Jeffrey Levett. 2013. "Relationship of Locus of Control, Psychological Distress and Trauma Exposure in Groups Impacted by Intense Political Conflict in Egypt." *Prehospital and Disaster Medicine* 28, no. 5: 423–27.

INDEX

Note: Numbers in italics denote figures.

3M Company 61–63, 83

Aalborg 133–34, 138, 146, 147, 151, 154
Aalborg University 133, 136, 165
Aarhus Museum of Art 137
Abramov, Maxim 45, 105
Acropolis (Greece) 187, 189
Aidareleyev, Asilbek 45, 56, 57–58
Ain Shams University (Cairo) 187
Akureyri (Iceland) 127
All-Women Expedition (AWE) (South Pole) (1992) 107–8
Amalienborg 125
American Association of University Women, College Park 10
American Joint Jewish Distribution Committee 73
Andersen, Hans Christian 147
Andreas (patrol chief) 125, 126, 128–31, 135
Antarctic research 157–64
Arab Spring study (Cairo) 188, 192, 195
Archangelsk (Soviet Union) 49, 53
Archangelsk Institute of Physiology (Ural) 38
Arkharov, Misha 52, 53, 62, 88
Arkharova, Nina 52
Armed Forces Radiobiology Research Institute (AFRRI) 62, 63
army psychiatrist, at hospital 4
Arnesen, Liv 119–21
Athens (Greece) 181–85, 187, 193–98

Athens National School of Public Health 167, *200*
Atlis, Mera 118, 119

Babi Yar 72
Baghat, Fahmy 184–85
Bancroft, Ann 107, 108, 119–21
Belarus Academy of Sciences 66
Belarus Institute of Physiology 66, 86, 87
Beliye Nochi (White Nights) 54
Bering Bridge dogsled and cross-country expedition (1989) 37, 38
Beringov Most (Bering Bridge) conference (1989) 39, 41
Bering Strait 37
binge eating 12
Blackadder-Weinstein, Jodie 157–63, *176*
Bondarenko, Dimitry 68
Brabec, Vladislav 80, 91
Bush, George H. W. 38
Butcher, J. 22, 23
Butcher, James (Jim) 68

C-130 Hercules cargo plane 145–46
Cairo (Egypt) 188, 192
Case Histories of Psychopathology (Leon) 31
case history book, writing 15
Center for Disaster Medicine (Moscow) 38
  Moscow trip to 39–43
center of competence 188

Charles, Dave 62–63
Chernobyl, journey to 68–73
Chernobyl explosion 54
Club Priklyucheniye (Adventure Club) 65, 88–89
College of Liberal Arts (CLA) (University of Minnesota) 21–23
communication, significance of 134
conflict resolution 155
Connors, Mary 62
Copenhagen (Denmark) 125
coping methods, psychologically adaptive 30
Corinth (Greece) 187
Corneliussen, Jesper 136–37, 139, 140, 142–48, 154, 165, *173*
Czech Labor Medicine Institute 80

Dahl, Liv 110–16
Daneborg station (2012) 123–35, 170, 171
Danish Arctic Command 124, 166
Delphi 184
Denmark (2012) 135–38
Donchenko, Adele 45
Dormidontov, Anatoly 45
Douglass College (Rutgers University, New Brunswick) 11, 18, 20

Eastern Psychological Association 15, 16, 18
Edvard Munch exhibition 137
Ellesmere Island (Canada) 111, 112, 116
Eriksen, Torben 123, 124, 125, 144, 165
Expedition Ice Maidens (England) (2018) and 157–64, *175*

Fink, Birgit 126–34, 136, 139, 144, 154–55, *170*, *171*
Fisher, Judith 162, 163
food consumption and regainers 12

Gadallah, Mohsen 187, 188, 189
Gallipoli (Istanbul) 190
Gavrilov, Alexei 66, 83
Gavrilov, Valentin 66, 86–88, 91
George, Anthony 162
Giannopoulou, Kalliopi 194

Glover, Ira 63
Gorbachev, Mikhail 38, 53, 57
Grechko, Stefan 85, 91
Greece 167, 179–80, 187–89
    Athens in 181–85, 187, 193, 193–98
    wildfires study in 167, 181, 191
Greenland trip
    Daneborg station (2012) and 123–35
    Denmark (2012) and 135–38
    Station Nord (2014) and 138–48
    Station Nord (2016) and 148–57
Grise Fiord (Canada) 110, 115, 116–17
Guscova, Angelina 67

Halpern, James 187, 188, 189, 195
Hamlyn Centre (England) 162
Harmon, Mark 39, 46
Have, Hans Christian 138–39, 166
Health Disaster Management 181
Hermitage museum (St. Petersburg) 75
Heroic Age of Antarctic Exploration 119
Hole, Lars 113, 114, *168*
Holland, Al 32, 51, 101
Holocaust survivors, coping and resilience of 24–27
Hourglass Bay (Canada) 111
Humans in Space Symposium (Cologne) 138
hygge 118

Iceland 126–27, 133, 149
Institute for Disaster Mental Health (SUNY New Paltz) 187
Institute of Clinical Radiology of Ukraine 68
Institute of Ecological Problems (Soviet Union) 54
International Atomic Energy Agency (IAEA) 62
International Date Line 37
International Workshop: Greece and Egypt (workshop) 187–88
Inupiat town 104
Iqaluit (Canada) 110, 117

INDEX 211

Ismailovo Park (Moscow) 86
Istanbul (Turkey) 189–90

Jesper, L. 151
Jihan, K. 184, 185

Kahn, Pauline Maki 107, 108
Kapor-Stanulovic, Nila 179
Karen Blixen (Isak Dinesen) 126
Keflavik 148–49
Keflavik Military Airport 145
Kenn Borek Air company 112
Kephalonia (Greece) 195–96
Khabarovsk (Soviet Union) 58
Kiev 68, 69, 72
Kjærgaard, Anders 124, 125, 126,
    133–39, 146–48, 151, 165, *172*, 201
komatik 115
Konstantinos 196
Kosorenko, Olga 51
Kostin, Vadim 39, 40, 45, 46, 47, 49, 53,
    55–56, 61–63, 65, 67, 70, 79–81,
    83, 84, 85, 89, 91, 92, 166–67
    death of 92
Kotzebue town 103, 104, 105
Kristina (Russian interpreter) 42, 50–51,
    53, 65, 67, 68, 70, 71, 73–75, 85

Laboratory for Health and Human
    Performance in Extreme
    Environments 92
Levett, Jeffery 167, 179–81, 183, 185,
    187, 188, 189, 191, 193, 194,
    195, 197
    International Gusi Peace Prize for 199
Livingston College (Rutgers
    University) 17
Lüscher Color Test 42

MACS-Delphi (Minnesota Advanced
    Cooling Suit-Delphi) 91
Magadan (Soviet Union) 49
    trip to 55–59
Magadan Institute of Biological
    Problems 38, 58
Magor, Graeme 109, 110, 115
Marathon (Athens) 197

Markov, Vasili 42, 50–52, 55, 66–70,
    74–76, 80, 85–89, 91, 92
Marya 49, 63, 67
Mayo Clinic 31
McMurdo Base 119
Mestervig Station (Greenland) 130–31
Michelle 46, 152
Midwest Psychological Association 20
Minneapolis Veteran Administration
    (VA) Hospital 23
Minnesota Multiphasic Personality
    Inventory (MMPI) 41, 46, 50, 51,
    63, 65, 67, 68, 80, 84, 86, 89, 91
Minsk trip 86–88
Mirella 185, 189, 193, 197
Moscow Institute of Emergency
    Children's Surgery and
    Traumatology 179–80
Moscow State University 42
Moscow trip
    in 1989 39–43
    in 1991 49–55
    in 1992 76, 79–80
    in 1994 85–86
Mousterakis, Theodore 194–95

NASA 32, 92, 144
    Ames Research Center (ARC) 62
    Human Research Program (HRP) 92,
        101, 138, 155–56, 201
    Johnson Space Center 51, 101
National Academy of Sciences
    32, 102
National Center for Social Solidarity
    (EKKA) (Greece) 194–95
National Institute of Child Health
    and Human Development
    (NICHD) 30
    five-year longitudinal project on eating
        disorders 30–31
National Institute of Environmental
    Health Sciences 83
National Institute of Mental Health
    (NIMH) 23, 83, 87
    research training grant from 31
National Opera and Ballet Theatre
    (Belarus) 88

National Organization for Women ((NOW) 18, 19
National School of Public Health (NSPH) 167, 180, 181, 191, 195, 196, 202
New York Times 19–20, *33*
Nobles, Raymond 19
Nome town 103–4
Norris, Rachel 157
Nuclear, Biological, Chemical (NBC) task force, WADEM 91

Odense 146, 147
Old Country Buffet 47

Papanikolaou, Basiliki "Vicky" 180, 181, 182, 187, 189, 191, 194, 195, 197
Patrice Lumumba University 68
Pavlov, Ivan 52, 76
Peloponnese peninsula 181
People's Friendship University 67
personal values, significance of 155
Petsetakis, Elisabeth 181
PhD certification
  requirements for 8
  significance of 8–10
Polina 49, 63
Popular Mechanics Magazine 123
Prehospital and Disaster Medicine (journal) 167
Pressler, Sylvia 18
Prince William Sound 105
Pripyat (Russia) 71
psychophysiology 52
Psychosocial Consequences of Natural Disasters (workshop) 183
psychosocial disaster workshops 167, 181–84, 195, *200*
psychosocial factors, theme of 188
Pyrros, Dimitry 188

Queen Maud Land 119

radiophobia 66
Rebecca 160, 161
Resolute (Canada) 110, 111–12, 115
Reykjavik (Iceland) 126, 127, 133, 149
Roberts, Paula 17–18, 19

Rønshøj, Kent 126, 166
Roshal, Leonid 179–80
Rosswork, Sandra 8
Roumelioti, Anastasia 188, 199
Royal Canadian Mounted Police 112
Royal Military Academy (Sandhurst) 158
Russian space program (Roscosmos) 62
Rutgers University
  New Brunswick campus 11, 12–13
  Newark campus 13–17
Ryazan trip 76–78

Sæmark-Thomsen, Bente 136
Sandal, Gro 119
Schurke, Paul 37–38, 42, 99, 104
Scientific Center of Radiation Medicine 66
  Kiev 69
  Moscow 66
sensed presence, phenomenon of 119, 120
sexist issues, for women 20
Shevchenko, Alex 61–62
Shparo, Dmitry 37, 38, 39, 42, 45, 46, 47, 65, 76, 77, 79, 88–89, 91, 95, 104
Shultz, James 183
Siberia 57
Sirius Patrol (Danish military) 123, 124, 125, 130, 133–39, 141, 142, 144, 145, 146, 148, 150
Skembris, Angelos 182, 193, 194, 195, 199
Smith, M. 160
social support, significance of 118
Sons of Norway 110
Soviet-American Bering Bridge Expedition 103–6
Søvik, Guldborg 113, 114, *168*
St. Petersburg 73–75
State University of New Jersey 19
Station Nord (Danish Military, Greenland) 137, 166, *172, 173, 175*
  2014, 138–48
  2016, 148–57
Steger, Will 99

Steger International Polar Expedition (1986) 37, 99–100
  network 101–2
Suedfeld, Peter 27
suit against discrimination at campus, for positions 17–20
Sverdrup, Otto 109
Sverdrup Centennial Expedition (Canada) (2000) 109–18, *168*
Sweasy, George 41, 46

Temple of Poseidon (Athens) 197
Tenyakshev, Alexander "Sasha" 39, 76, 77
Title IX, of Education Amendments (1972) 17–18
Tkachev, Anatoly 45, 53, 54, 62, 85, 92, 93
Treviño, Robert 91
Troelsgaard, Marie 148–54
Tsyvilko (Professor) 67
Turkey 189–90
Twin Otter flight 112, 117, 127
two-woman Antarctic traverse (2000) 119–21

Ukrainian National Chernobyl Museum (Kiev) 72
United States Public Health Service 11
University of Maryland 7
  Overseas Extension Division (France) 3
University of Miami School of Medicine 183

University of Minnesota 12, 19, 20, 21, 32, 38, 43, 91, 202
  Bering Bridge Conference 45–47
  College of Liberal Arts (CLA) 21–23
  Division of Environmental and Occupational Health (EOH) 63
  Press 50, 67, 68, 84
  When Everyone Leaves conference (1996) 91
University of North Dakota 161
US Army Research Institute of Environmental Medicine (USARIEM) 38, 46, 104
US Equal Employment Opportunity Commission (EEOC) 17, 18
USSR Center for Preventive Medicine (Moscow) 52

Valdez town 105
Vietnam-era nurses (VN-E), coping of 28–29
Vietnam Women's Memorial Project 28

Walder, Leo 7, 10
Walter Reed Army Institute of Research 7
Weight Watchers (New Jersey) 11
WinSCAT tool 141, 142, 144
Withnall, Rich 161
World Association of Disaster and Emergency Medicines (WADEM) 91, 162, 166–67, 188, 194
  Health Disaster Management Guidelines for Evaluation and Research 179
  psychosocial taskforce 91, 167

www.ingramcontent.com/pod-product-compliance
Lightning Source LLC
Chambersburg PA
CBHW032023230426
43671CB00005B/179